AIDS AND THE LAW

AIDS AND THE LAW
A Basic Guide for the Nonlawyer

Allan H. Terl

●HEMISPHERE PUBLISHING CORPORATION
A member of the Taylor & Francis Group

Washington   Philadelphia   London

AIDS AND THE LAW: A Basic Guide for the Nonlawyer

Copyright © 1992 by Hemisphere Publishing Corporation. All rights reserved.
Printed in the United States of America. Except as permitted under the United
States Copyright Act of 1976, no part of this publication may be reproduced or
distributed in any form or by any means, or stored in a database or retrieval
system, without the prior written permission of the publisher.

1 2 3 4 5 6 7 8 9 0   B R B R   9 8 7 6 5 4 3 2

This book was set in Century by Hemisphere Publishing Corporation. The editors
were Amy Lyles Wilson and Becky Reynolds; the production supervisor was
Peggy M. Rote; and the typesetter was Darrell D. Larsen, Jr. Cover design by
Sharon M. DePass.
Printing and binding by Braun-Brumfield, Inc.

A CIP catalog record for this book is available from the British Library.

Library of Congress Cataloging-in-Publication Data

Terl, Allan H.
    AIDS and the law: a basic guide for the nonlawyer / by Allan H.
Terl.
        p. cm.
    Includes bibliographical references.
    1. AIDS (Disease)—Law and legislation—United States. I. Title.
    KF3803.A54T47   1992
    344.73'04369792—dc20
    [347.3044369792]   91-38449
                                                                    CIP

ISBN 1-56032-218-7 (cloth)
ISBN 1-56032-219-5 (paper)

In memory of Bud, Tommy, Jim, Al, Richard, Ivan, Lee, Todd, Charlie, Jack, Gabe, Jay, Thomas, Terry, Dana, Eddie, Carl, Lon, and too many others.

Contents

Acknowledgments

The author gratefully acknowledges his heavy reliance on the AIDS and Civil Liberties Project of the American Civil Liberties Union; *AIDS Update,* a publication of Lambda Legal Defense and Education Fund, Inc.; and the *AIDS Litigation Reporter,* published by Andrews Publications.

The author also thanks the Fort Lauderdale, Florida, office of the Social Security Administration for its guidance on substantive matters; the Stonewall Library and Archives for its availability of back documents; friends Linda C. Abbott, Laura Z. Stuurmans, Walter Lindberg, and George Van Lanen for their persistent rescue of a computer-illiterate author; and the author's best clipping services, his sisters Phyll and Fran.

Finally, the author expresses his sincere thanks to his editor, Amy Lyles Wilson, for her most constructive and thoughtful assistance with this work.

Preface

The inquiries come in at an average rate of 15 to 20 a week. Most are by telephone; a few are by direct mail; more than a few are referrals from the state or local ACLU offices; and those are all in addition to the questions fielded at lectures at AIDS social service centers or from students or others before whom I lecture.

Most often the questions come from persons with AIDS (PWAs). They have had their health insurance companies refuse to pay a claim or otherwise try to avoid covering their medical expenses. Some come from persons who have been recently diagnosed as HIV-positive and who are worried about their rights to keep their jobs. Others come from lovers or family members who are worried about creditors taking away their property.

The nature of the inquiries shifts from time to time—from an area that becomes relatively settled, such as employment discrimination against PWAs, to such new issues as the right to know whether one's doctor or dentist carries the AIDS virus. Shift though they may, the settled issues continue to resurface, and new twists to old issues arise with regularity.

Too few of the inquiries come from employers seeking to understand their obligations to employees with HIV disease or seeking to help them keep such employees in the work force and, in the process, keep them insured. Too few come from people seeking to open housing opportunities to people with HIV disease and who, because of depletion of funds or prejudice, have lost their homes. Too few come from school administrators or teachers or parents seeking to help students or others understand each other's rights. Too few come from unions seeking to go to bat for members with HIV disease.

The first call on this issue was not to me but from me. It was made by me in my capacity as a leader of a then-fledgling local chapter of the ACLU. It was made in response to a small item in the local newspaper relating the story of a budget analyst with the county budget office who was fired only and specifically because he had been diagnosed with AIDS. By the end of that day, the fired budget analyst had become a client of our ACLU chapter. The case that ensued generated the first ruling in the country that AIDS is a handicapping condition entitling a person with AIDS to the benefits of laws protecting against discrimination on the basis of handicap.

As an advocate for the rights of persons with AIDS, I received hate calls and threats. As an attorney who had focused his career on such people-oriented issues as consumerism and civil rights, I became all the more determined to do my part to help establish the rights of people with AIDS and to help the public understand those rights. Moreover, the opportunity to help shape the direction of a new area of law was and remains an exciting career opportunity with which an attorney is rarely presented.

Just as there are rights involved, so too are there liabilities involved. For those who discriminate unlawfully—whether in employment, housing, public accommodations, government services, or other areas—there are serious penalties. For those who violate other AIDS-related laws, there may even be criminal penalties. For those who ignore others' rights, there is often also resulting heartbreak and guilt even beyond legal liability.

This volume is written in the hope that an understanding of the legal issues relating to HIV disease will help those with specific rights to be aware of them, to muster the courage to insist on them and, if necessary, to pursue them through the courts. It is written in the hope of avoiding unnecessary infringement on those rights and liability for those who do infringe them because of ignorance of these legal rights. Most of all, it is written in the hope that those outside the legal profession—those too often perplexed by what seems to them to be confusing legal mumbo-jumbo—will be able to understand the broad scope of our legal system as it interplays with the issues raised by this still fairly new phenomenon called AIDS.

Introduction

The need for a book on AIDS and the law for nonlawyers may at first puzzle some people who quite logically feel that legal issues should be left to lawyers. And though they are generally right as to the trial of these issues within the legal system, a wide variety of people within our society should understand at least the basics of these legal issues.

For those who have not yet grasped the magnitude of what we as a human race face from this tragedy, let me relate recent statistics and predictions. On the continent where many believe that the Acquired Immune Deficiency Syndrome (AIDS) has its roots, AIDS is said to be "galloping across Africa, killing up to a third of the adult population in some areas, and leaving thousands of orphans, including many infected with the virus."[1] Projections by the U.S. Bureau of the Census forecast that by 2015 "there will be more than 70 million cases of AIDS in the countries south of the Sahara Desert" with "AIDS-related infections already represent[ing] up to 80% of the hospital admissions in Zambia."[2]

As the Seventh International Conference on AIDS

opened in Florence in June 1991, African and Asian countries pleaded for more help from richer nations.[3] United Nations officials were predicting that the AIDS virus could infect 40 million people by the end of the century.[4] A study released in August 1991 said that AIDS is spreading so rapidly in Africa that the worst-affected areas will show a net population loss within a few decades.[5]

Closer to home, the Pan American Health Organization estimates that "more than three million people in the Western Hemisphere will be infected with the AIDS virus by the mid-1990s," with about two million people in North and South America already infected.[6]

But still, aren't the populations in Africa and South America very different in culture and state of medical care than what we have here in the United States? This isn't something that could really happen here, is it? Sadly, it not only could happen, but it's already well under way.

Federal health officials estimate that one million Americans are already infected with human immunodeficiency virus (HIV), the virus believed to be the cause of AIDS.[7] The U.S. Centers for Disease Control (CDC) has predicted that of these, an estimated 165,000 to 215,000 will die during 1991–1993.[8]

As of June 1990, the U.S. death toll from AIDS had already surpassed 83,000—more than the number of Americans who died in battle in the Vietnam and Korean wars combined.[9] A short seven months later, the death toll from AIDS in the United States had topped 100,000, with nearly a third of the deaths occurring in the prior year and with the rate escalating.[10] AIDS had by then become the second leading cause of death among American men between 25 and 44, second only to accidental injuries.[11] AIDS is already the leading cause of death for men between 25 and 44 in New York City, Los Angeles, and San Francisco, and for black women between 15 and 44 in New York state and New Jersey.[12]

But aren't we talking about promiscuous gay men and intravenous drug users who share needles? Aren't those the groups to which AIDS has really been confined?

Even if we were talking about a medical phenomenon

that strikes only those groups—and surely we are not—those populations have legal rights relating to education, employment, insurance, housing, and the full range of issues that touch the population as a whole.

It is important to understand that the time for any such stereotyping of populations at risk for AIDS is long gone. Although it may have appeared first in those populations in the United States, HIV is now an equal-opportunity virus. HIV spread rapidly in the initially infected populations because there was little recognition or acceptance of the methods that spread the virus while that process was happening, and now other populations are experiencing explosive increases in numbers of HIV infections as they persist in the erroneous belief that it can't happen to them.

Primary among these newly affected populations are heterosexual women, according to various studies released at the Sixth International Conference on AIDS, held in San Francisco in June 1990. One study found that women are the fastest-growing group in the country infected with HIV, with their numbers having increased by 45% in the single year prior to the study.[13] The death rate from AIDS among women quadrupled from 1985 to 1988, and AIDS became the leading cause of death for women between 25 and 34 in New York City.[14] The study released in August 1991 made clear that the primary means of transmission of HIV in the drastically affected African populations is heterosexual sex.[15]

According to the CDC, 31% of the more than 13,600 American women with AIDS as of that conference got the disease through heterosexual intercourse.[16] And in a manner similar to that attitude initially expressed by the other populations that AIDS hit so heavily, a study by the Johns Hopkins School of Medicine in Baltimore found that women did not believe they were at risk. "More than 40% of the women now infected did not know that they had engaged in high-risk behavior," with the problem compounded by physicians' failures to diagnose AIDS in women because the physicians do not think of it as a women's disease.[17]

No, AIDS knows nothing about whether one is male or female, straight or gay, an intravenous drug abuser or avoider of aspirin, a believer in God or an atheist. It knows not whether one is a prostitute of either sex, a sexually experimenting teenager, the faithful spouse or one not so faithful, or an innocent newborn. HIV is a virus—plain and simple—and given the opportunity for transmission, it is transmitted all too often.

Why, then, should legal issues be of interest unless one is directly affected because of being infected?

The answer revolves around the single word "discrimination" as it relates to treatment of one who is possibly infected with HIV, that person's family members, and that person's ability to earn a living, remain insured, and maintain some semblance of privacy about his or her life.

The word "discrimination" is itself repugnant to many, but it should not be. Discrimination is simply the making of a choice. Each of us discriminates many times each day—in deciding which clothes to wear, which foods to eat, which manner of transportation to use, which stores to patronize, and so on. It is simply a manner of favoring one possible alternative over another—of choosing, of preferring, or not treating equally. There is obviously nothing unlawful or even immoral about that. It is a very natural part of life.

Discrimination takes on a different character, however, when it is exercised against people. Our nation is built on the precept of equality, as evidenced in both the Declaration of Independence and the Constitution. Indeed, the inscription above the entrances to the Supreme Court Building, which houses the ultimate arbiter of decisions within our judicial branch of government, proclaims for all to see: EQUAL JUSTICE UNDER LAW.

The concept of equality under law doesn't negate our abilities or our rights to make everyday choices or even personally to prefer some people over others for certain purposes. But that same principle of equality does require that our government and society as a whole eliminate institutional discrimination on bases declared to be unlawful.

It is when the principle of equality is breached in that manner that government has a proper role and one that it has, in fact, undertaken—albeit grudgingly at times. Laws attempting to effectuate equality date most apparently to the Emancipation Proclamation—an attempt that was not quite a law, with freedom from slavery also being far from today's concept of equality. In 1896, the U.S. Supreme Court still felt that separate facilities could be equal for persons of different colors,[18] and not until the 1948 presidential campaign and the *Brown v. Board of Education* decision in 1954[19] did modern-day civil rights really begin to come of age.

Under our system of government, the primary role for protecting the principle of equality rests with the legislative branch, and Congress finally exerted leadership on this issue in 1964. The 1964 Civil Rights Act[20] meant for many the awakening of the American conscience as it made unlawful discrimination on the bases of race, color, national origin, and religion in such areas as employment, public accommodations, and federally assisted programs. Thereafter, Congress allowed (or perhaps invited) a piecemeal approach and systematically enacted laws protecting people in varying degrees from discrimination on the bases of sex, age, and handicap.

The common feature that underlies the notion that discrimination should be unlawful is a group's natural status. Each protected category is not a matter of choice but is dictated by one's inherited or involuntarily acquired traits. The one possible exception is religion, as to which one really does have a choice, but which is traditionally an inherited characteristic and which has also been afforded particularly special protection under our Constitution since the First Amendment was ratified.

It is with that background in mind that we turn to a much closer examination of just one aspect of discrimination on the basis of handicap. As with other areas of discrimination, handicap is not a matter of choice. Thus, Congress and the individual states acted to curb discrimination against those who are handicapped and who may, therefore, need special protection under the law. The landmark legislation was the Rehabilitation Act of 1973, the most pertinent provision of which is known as "Section 504."[21]

Concerns about handicap discrimination at first focused on curb cuts (so that those who are wheelchair-bound could maneuver without the traditional barriers presented by something as simple to the rest of us as a curb), on braille elevator directions, on wheelchair lifts for public transportation, on restroom facilities specially designed for the handicapped, and on reading machines or assistants for the visually impaired. Sign language interpreters became an accepted part of public meetings.

But about a decade after the Rehabilitation Act was enacted, a strange new phenomenon appeared on the American scene. Just as the prohibition against discrimination on the basis of handicap was gaining widespread popular acceptance, young men began contracting cancers and pneumonias that had usually been reserved for the elderly or for people from distant lands. AIDS went quickly from phenomenon to theory to definable medical condition.

Those of us within the network of HIV/AIDS service organizations immediately recognized discrimination on the basis of HIV status as discrimination on the basis of handicap. Others, however, sought in legal terms to invoke the police and public health powers of government; in less legal terms, they feared for their health and safety and wanted to be protected from the threat they perceived. In some cases, AIDS provided a convenient excuse for people to exercise their deep-seated prejudices against gays, people dependent upon drugs, prostitutes, and other less mainstream, less politically powerful groups who were the earliest, unsuspecting targets of HIV infection.

These fears and prejudices led to a wide variety of proposals to deal with HIV issues, and the intent of this book is to provide a perspective on how we as a society and our governments at their several levels have dealt with these issues. In a little more than a decade since AIDS was really defined with any precision, some of these issues have been resolved; others are just beginning to emerge.

In its 1990 report "Epidemic of Fear," the AIDS Project of the American Civil Liberties Union reached several pertinent conclusions about HIV infection and discrimination. Reported cases of AIDS-related discrimination increased by about 50%, it said, and rose 35% faster than newly diagnosed AIDS cases in 1988.[22] Moreover, nearly one-third of all reported discrimination cases were based solely on the perception that someone was HIV-positive or because of association with HIV-positive persons.[23] Insurance, housing, and health care represented about one-third of the complaints, with 37% relating to employment and employment discrimination often overlapping with insurance, health care, and public accommodations issues.[24] The report added its voice to those of us pleading for the public and policymakers to understand that AIDS and AIDS discrimination cut across lines of race, gender, sexual orientation, and ethnicity.[25] It pointed out quite correctly that because of advances in treatment, people with HIV diseases will continue to live longer with their illnesses, will be vulnerable to HIV-related discrimination for longer periods of time, and will likely suffer a greater volume of unfair treatment. Those affected by discrimination, it pointed out, are therefore apt to be healthier, less inclined to think of themselves as "dying," and more determined to retain the full quality of life in terms of housing, the workplace, and public accommodations.[26]

This work leaves to others the explanations of how the virus transmits, reproduces, and conquers its new hosts' immune systems. Our concern here is the myriad legal issues that face those with the virus and those with any kind of relationship—or even just the possibility of a relationship—to those with the virus. It offers neither the precision nor the documentation of a traditional legal treatise, and it does not pretend to be such. It does not treat all of the cases on any particular subtopic. This work avoids technical legal issues and jurisdictional fights between states or between state and federal courts; it focuses instead on substantive legal issues in nontechnical language so that the nonlawyer can understand and relate to the issues discussed.

In May 1991, the World Health Organization predicted that HIV will infect as many as 30 million adults and ten million children by the end of the century. That total is about ten million higher than the United Nations agency's estimate just a year earlier.[27] For the United States, the director of the AIDS Program at the Centers for Disease Control predicted in June 1991, on the tenth anniversary of the first public report of the syndrome, that more than 500,000 Americans will be stricken with AIDS in the next ten years.[28]

This work is aimed at everyone from the person with AIDS (PWA) to coworkers of PWAs, employers of PWAs, and employees of PWAs; from school administrators and teachers to students attending classes with PWAs and families of children attending classes with HIV-infected youngsters or even those only thought to be; from hospital administrators and health-care workers to health-care industry volunteers; from high-level policymakers within government to sympathetic or even merely curious next-door neighbors. With predictions as staggering as those from the World Health Organization and the Centers for Disease Control, all of us have a role with regard to AIDS as it affects increasingly large and diverse segments of society, and all have an interest in understanding legal issues that could have ramifications for those with HIV disease—for that could easily be any one of us.

NOTES

1. "Africa in Grip of Decimating AIDS Spread," *The Miami Herald,* February 17, 1991, p. 31A.

2. *Id.*

3. "Asians, Africans ask for AIDS help," *Fort Lauderdale Sun-Sentinel,* June 17, 1991, p. 5A.

4. *Id.*

5. "Study: AIDS to Wipe Out Some African Populations," a Reuters story appearing in the *Fort Lauderdale Sun-Sentinel,* August 15, 1991, p. 15A.

6. "3 Million May Have AIDS by Mid-'90s," an Associated Press story appearing in *Fort Lauderdale Sun-Sentinel,* March 11, 1990, p. 3A.

7. "U.S. Death Toll from AIDS Passes 100,000," an Associated

Press story appearing in *The Miami Herald*, January 25, 1991, p. 12A.

8. *Id.*

9. *The Miami Herald*, June 19, 1990, p. 2A.

10. "100,000 Have Died of AIDS," *Fort Lauderdale Sun-Sentinel*, January 25, 1991, p. 3A.

11. *Id.*

12. *The Advocate*, No. 571 (February 26, 1991), p. 26.

13. "Women Stalked by AIDS," *The Miami Herald*, June 24, 1990, p. 1A.

14. *Id.*

15. See n. 5, *supra.*

16. See n. 13, *supra.*

17. *Id.*

18. *Plessey v. Ferguson*, 163 U.S. 537 (1896).

19. *Brown v. Board of Education*, 347 U.S. 483 (1954).

20. Pub. Law 88-352.

21. 29 U.S.C. Sect. 794.

22. See *AIDS Lit. Rptr.*, August 10, 1990, p. 4909.

23. *Id.*

24. *Id.*

25. *Id.*

26. *Id.*

27. "WHO Predicts 40 Million HIV Infections by 2000," an Associated Press story appearing in *The Weekly News*, May 8, 1991, p. 30.

28. "AIDS Program Chief Sees 500,000 New Cases by 2001," a Reuters story appearing in the *Fort Lauderdale Sun-Sentinel*, June 6, 1991, p. 10A.

1

The Early Legislative Quick Fixes

From the beginning of the AIDS crisis, some states acted reasonably and compassionately. Most notably, New York, California, and Wisconsin did not allow fear or prejudice to rush them into foolish or discriminatory practices. Others, like Florida, took just a bit longer, and after a little prodding, finally developed highly responsible and comprehensive policies regarding HIV disease.

Still other states, however, reacted to AIDS as the wagon trains of the pioneer days did in response to approaching Indians—form the wagons into a circle and just keep shooting until the perceived menace is destroyed, contained, or forced to retreat. The psychological framework of those involved on any facet of this issue today can be more easily understood if one looks briefly at some of the products of the "circle-the-wagons" mentality.

In Colorado, a legislative proposal would have required HIV-antibody testing of persons "reasonably believed" to have AIDS or to have been exposed to HIV.[1] Can we guess who would have been "reasonably believed" to have been exposed? The measure would have allowed quarantine of individuals and required mandatory reporting of HIV-positive persons. The bill was amended on the Senate floor to include provisions encouraging public education and information. Ironically, that amendment was unacceptable to the bill's sponsor, who then withdrew it from consideration. Yes, any legislator can sponsor a bill, and state legislatures are full of them on the extremes of the political spectrum. What is significant about this Colorado bill is that it was not an off-the-wall action of some kooky legislator that would generate a flashy headline and then die a quick legislative death. At the time of the Colorado Senate's action, the bill had already passed the Colorado House of Representatives!

In another example of this circle-the-wagons mentality, a series of bills in Idaho precluded persons with AIDS from many activities.[2] That state made it a felony for a known infected individual to engage in any "crime against nature" (the traditional code legal phrase for sodomy) that would cause another to become infected. It applied to not only those with AIDS and AIDS-Related Complex (ARC), a stage of HIV disease short of full AIDS, but also to those with "a significant likelihood of carrying" the HIV infection. Again, we know who those people are!

Other Idaho legislation would have required school officials to exclude "infected" pupils and made unlawful the employment as a teacher or school staff any person with AIDS or a related infection. Idaho's reaction also included legislation to make it a criminal misdemeanor for an "infected" child to attend day care or for an "infected" adult to offer day-care services. And yet another bill sought to proscribe "infected" persons from conducting, operating, or being employed in any eating establishment. And once again it is appropriate to note that any legislator—even one whose outlook may be out of step with others' thinking—can sponsor legislation. The frightening reality of these bills, however, is that they were all enacted into law![3]

In California, a group called Prevent AIDS Now Initiative Committee (PANIC) successfully petitioned to the ballot a proposal to subject persons with HIV disease in any stage to quarantine and isolation. Those only suspected of being infected would have been barred from food-service jobs and schools. The measure was overwhelmingly defeated at the polls.[4]

And stupidity is not limited to the states. U.S. Representative Dan Burton filed a bill to require each state to test annually all residents for HIV and to counsel those found to be positive for the virus. If the state didn't comply with the requirement, it would forfeit its federal reimbursement under the Social Security Act.[5]

My favorite example by far, however, of the early political hysteria generated by the arrival of AIDS was a Utah legislative product. In 1987, that state enacted a law prohibiting and declaring void any marriage to a person with AIDS.[6] "Void" means that no marriage to a PWA could be legal. A marriage that already existed and in which one party had AIDS was dissolved by operation of law! I've always wondered just exactly when the "void" status attached—retroactively to the point of infection, at the point of AIDS diagnosis, or when? In addition to the rights of the parties to the marriage, the results of a marriage becoming void by operation of a law such as this raises very serious questions of the legitimacy of children.

So much for the mindset that HIV disease generated when it first appeared as a new threat to human health. Let us now turn to specific areas of law and examine the kinds of problems that have arisen with regard to AIDS and how the law has dealt with them.

NOTES

1. See *AIDS Update*, Lambda Legal Defense and Education Fund, Inc., No. 7 (June 1986), pp. 1–2.

2. *Ibid.*, pp. 3–4.

3. *Id.*

4. See *AIDS Update*, Lambda Legal Defense and Education Fund, Inc., No. 12 (November 1986), p. 10.

5. See *AIDS Update*, Lambda Legal Defense and Education Fund, Inc., No. 18 (May 1987), p. 11.

6. Chapter 246, Section 1, Laws of 1987, codified at Section 30-1-2, Utah Code Ann. (1989).

2

Access to Justice

Some may initially wonder why there should even be a concern about persons with HIV disease having access to justice. Everyone has access to justice, or so goes the American ideal.

But as we shall see throughout this volume, HIV disease is unlike any other illness with which our modern society has ever dealt. The degree of ignorance in society is high, and the degree of fear even higher. The justice system, after all, is run by people who are all too subject to that ignorance and those fears.

Moreover, persons with HIV disease have special problems that they bring to the legal system. And the system may indeed really be trying to provide such persons with an equal opportunity at fairness by giving them a helping hand in order to equalize their chance at justice with the chance enjoyed by persons not infected with HIV.

The courts have been slow in recognizing these special problems. In April 1989, the State Justice Institute and the National Institute of Justice co-sponsored a national conference on AIDS. Some 250 state court judges, court administrators, lawyers, doctors, and advocates of the rights of PWAs attended and discussed pertinent issues. Among the issues were protecting the privacy of PWAs as weighed against the need to protect the public from transmission of HIV; balancing risks to the defendant and the public in determining the sentence for a PWA convicted of a crime; dealing with fears of court personnel about courtroom contact with PWAs; and introducing new aspects of old issues of discrimination in employment, housing, public accommodations, and schools.[1] Even beyond the 250 attendees at the conference, a full issue of *The Judges' Journal* was devoted to "The Challenge AIDS Poses to the Courts" so as to reach the multitude of judges who were not in attendance at the conference.[2]

New York Supreme Court Justice Richard T. Andrias, a leader in the effort to educate judges about HIV disease, points to inconclusive reports during the mid-1980s on the methods of transmission of the AIDS virus as a significant reason for public alarm about infection by mere casual contact.[3] Fears of contagion are even stronger among criminal justice personnel because of the high incidence of intravenous drug use among criminal defendants.[4] Andrias joins in the recommendations of the American Bar Association[5] in calling for HIV education of all criminal justice system personnel and detainees, after which "the twin goals of safety and fairness can be advanced in an atmosphere free from tension and anxiety."[6]

Some court systems have dealt responsibly with these issues. In mid-1990, for example, the Chief Justice of the Delaware Supreme Court issued a comprehensive administrative directive providing that the HIV status of litigants and court staff should remain confidential and not made a part of any court proceeding in the state's court system. Under the directive, HIV status cannot be a basis for denying or limiting a defendant's access to the courtroom or a reason for avoiding court appearances.[7]

Many of the access-to-justice problems faced by persons with HIV disease in the criminal justice system are addressed with some specificity in Chapter 6. The number of cases involving charges stemming from biting, spitting, and other kinds of assaults cannot help but intimidate court personnel who could easily be subject to the same antisocial behavior by one already before the courts and hostile to the system because of pending criminal charges. One case discussed in Chapter 6 deals with a negative result to an HIV-antibody test being required as a condition to release on bond.[8] Another involves the overturning of a conviction because of possible jury prejudice in which court personnel unnecessarily wore gloves when dealing with an HIV-infected defendant.[9]

In one of the worst examples of court discrimination against someone with HIV disease, a defendant in a Florida traffic court hearing in March 1989 entered a no-contest plea, after which his father asked the judge for leniency in sentencing because his son was sick. The judge insisted on knowing the nature of the illness and, when advised by a written note from the defendant that said "AIDS," the judge ordered the defendant removed from the courtroom, directed everyone else to vacate the room, and went to her chambers, refusing to return to the courtroom until a bailiff had cleaned off her bench. She explained by saying, "I was very shocked. I touched the guy. I don't know if he has open sores or what. I have hangnails. . . . For 250 people to be exposed to someone, it's not fair."[10] A formal complaint filed against that judge ultimately resulted in the gag rule prohibiting public discussion of complaints against Florida judges being declared unconstitutional as an abridgement of the rights to free speech in the First Amendment.[11] Incidentally, for whatever reasons, the judge resigned from the bench within a matter of months after this incident.

As recently as June 1991, a similar incident occurred in California when a municipal court judge ordered his courtroom disinfected after an appearance by a man infected with the AIDS virus.[12]

Other cases have arisen on the civil side of legal proceedings. In what is believed to have been the first victory in an AIDS-related employment discrimination case in Oregon, the court awarded legal fees of approximately double what would be the usual rate. The court cited both the difficulty of the case and the need to encourage attorneys to accept such cases.[13]

Several cases have demonstrated the need for the judicial system to accommodate the shorter life expectancy of persons with HIV disease. In her well-known suit against the Florida dentist from whom she alleged that she contracted HIV, Kimberly Bergalis was allowed to videotape her testimony because of fears that she might die before the suit would be tried.[14] (Ms. Bergalis has since died.) And an HIV-positive former employee was granted an expedited trial in his $5 million discrimination and harassment suit against his former employer.[15]

The American Bar Association's (ABA) Policy on AIDS sets forth principles on this issue of access to justice:

- The judiciary and the organized bar should encourage attorneys and judges to become knowledgeable about HIV and related legal issues, and should provide appropriate education and training in these areas.
- The judiciary and the organized bar should support the allocation of additional private and public resources, including the further development of *pro bono* [at no charge] activities, for the delivery of legal services to individuals affected by HIV.
- An attorney should not refuse to represent or limit or modify representation because of an individual's known or perceived HIV status.
- A judicial or administrative proceeding involving a participant known or perceived to be HIV-infected should be conducted in the same fashion as any other such proceeding. Extraordinary safety or security precautions should not be undertaken based solely upon the participant's known or perceived HIV status.[16]

Specifically as to the criminal justice system, the ABA added to its overall AIDS policy, as well as to the already noted recommendation regarding education of justice system personnel, a further caution. "Where a court has determined that a defendant's HIV status is relevant in a criminal case," the ABA said, "the court must be provided with the most current, accurate, and objective medical information about a defendant's condition."[17] Moreover, "[u]nless the defendant's HIV status is at issue in the prosecution, only those with a demonstratable need or right to know should receive medical information about a defendant's HIV status. Criminal justice personnel who receive such information must safeguard its confidentiality."[18]

We have all heard of so-called "hanging judges," and it is, of course, up to each judge to determine how tough he or she will be in any particular circumstance regarding persons who are or may be HIV-positive or HIV-negative. But hopefully, we will not again hear of a judge acting in the HIV-ignorant manner as did the "hangnail judge" in Florida.

NOTES

1. Torbert, C. C., Jr., "The Challenge AIDS Poses to the Courts," *The Judges' Journal,* Vol. 29, No. 2 (Spring 1990), p. 2.

2. *The Judges' Journal,* Vol. 29, No. 2 (Spring 1990).

3. Andrias, Justice Richard T., "Shed Your Robes," *The Judges' Journal,* Vol. 29, No. 2 (Spring 1990), p. 4.

4. *Ibid.,* p. 5.

5. "Policy on AIDS and the Criminal Justice System," adopted by the House of Delegates of the American Bar Association, February 7, 1989.

6. Andrias, *loc. cit.*

7. Administrative Directive No. 84, DE Sup. Ct., July 2, 1990. See *AIDS Lit. Rptr.,* July 27, 1990, p. 4824.

8. See Chapter 6, "Criminal Law," n. 45.

9. *Ibid.,* n. 49.

10. Branham, Lynn S., "AIDS Before the Bench," *The Judges' Journal,* Vol. 29., No. 2, p. 47.

11. See Chapter 10, "Free Speech," n. 2.

12. "Fearing AIDS, Judge Has Courtroom Cleaned," *The Miami Herald,* June 15, 1991, p. 7A.

13. *Griffin v. Tri-Met et al.,* OR App. Ct., No. A64191. See *AIDS Lit. Rptr.,* May 25, 1990, p. 4549.

14. "Video Testimony OKd in AIDS Case," *The Miami Herald,* August 30, 1990, p. 7BR.

15. *Herbert v. Amrex-Zetron et al.,* CA Super. Ct., Los Angeles Cty., No. C 709 912. See *AIDS Lit. Rptr.,* November 9, 1990, p. 5338.

16. "Policy on AIDS," adopted by the American Bar Association, August 1989.

17. "Policy on AIDS and the Criminal Justice System," *supra.*

18. *Id.*

3

Public Benefits

Several kinds of important public benefits may be available to persons with HIV disease. This author can personally recall that in the early days of AIDS, workers at the offices of the Social Security Administration (SSA) would encourage applicants to obtain their application forms by telephone request and to submit them by mail. There were periodic reports of Social Security staff being, shall we say, less than interested in having PWAs in their offices.

Education of both the general public and the federal work force has, however, seemingly changed those attitudes, and one seldom hears such stories any longer. Rather, we now hear of very compassionate Social Security employees who are fully willing to work with those with HIV disease to help determine eligibility for benefits and to help applicants maximize their range of benefits available.

The two basic kinds of benefits with which anyone interested in HIV disease should be familiar are Social Security Disability Income (SSD) and Supplemental Security Income (SSI). SSD is very much like any insurance program. So long as one has paid sufficiently into the system through typical payroll deductions for Social Security, then the SSD benefits are payable when one becomes "disabled." Special provisions allow children, surviving spouses, or in some cases even grandchildren to collect SSD. There is a waiting period, with benefits starting for the sixth month after the date that the evidence shows the applicant became disabled.[1]

SSI, on the other hand, is realistically more of a welfare-type program. It is need-based, with the determining criteria involving the applicant's income and assets. Paid from federal general revenues rather than the Social Security trust funds, SSI eligibility requires no prior work with payments into the Social Security system and no waiting period.[2]

Those with documented AIDS, who are not working and who meet the other requirements for Social Security coverage, generally qualify as sufficiently "disabled." These benefits may also sometimes be payable for those with ARC. Applications by persons with ARC are evaluated on a case-by-case basis. If the applicant's condition is so severe that he or she is unable to work, then "disabled" status is generally found.[3]

As further evidence of the cooperative attitude now generally seen from the SSA regarding HIV-related claims, the administration has issued to medical professionals a guide explaining what medical evidence should be presented in support of one's claim for "disabled" status and the attendant benefits.[4] Moreover, the entire application process can be taken care of by phone or mail as well as in person at a Social Security office.[5]

These programs become all the more important because qualification for SSD generally entitles one to the benefits of Medicare after a requisite two-year period of receipt of SSD benefits has passed, and qualification for SSI generally entitles one to the benefits of Medicaid and food stamps.

Should you apply for either SSD or SSI and be denied those benefits, you do have a right to appeal the denial. In many instances, local offices operating under the authority of the Legal Services Corporation, law school clinical programs, or comparable entities offer to those who qualify for their services free legal representation on appeals of these denials. The qualification for their services is usually indigency, and those applying for SSD or SSI are often eligible for the no-cost legal services as well.

While there are a great many cases regarding denials of individuals' claims for either SSI or SSD, one case of particular significance has arisen in this area. In late 1990, a class action suit was filed in New York charging that many HIV-infected minorities, women, and children are denied federal disability benefits because they don't exhibit symptoms that fit into eligibility criteria established by the Centers for Disease Control. Those criteria, which would generally form the basis for the criteria used by the SSA, are alleged to be tailored generally to middle-class, gay males.[6] This case takes on added significance in light of the demographics related in the Introduction to this book, indicating that the infection rate among women is multiplying as the infection rate among gay males declines.

Perhaps in response to the issues raised in the class action suit, the Centers for Disease Control has revised its definition of AIDS. Effective January 1992, AIDS can be diagnosed on the basis of a blood count—specifically a count of what are known as T-cells, which should eliminate any definitional bias in favor of or against any particular group.[7] That does not mean, however, that the definition has been changed for all purposes, and the SSA's definition of AIDS for the purpose of determining eligibility for disability benefits has not kept pace with the CDC change as of this writing.

The SSA has done a fine job of summarizing eligibility criteria and application procedures for both SSI and SSD. Anyone interested may call a local Social Security office or write to the Social Security Administration at Baltimore, Maryland 21235 and request the most recent publications on SSD and SSI.

NOTES

1. "Social Security Disability Programs," SSA Publication No. 05-10057 (March 1991).

2. *Id.*

3. See "AIDS/ARC and Social Security," Atlanta Factsheet/No. 1, published by the Public Affairs Office, Social Security Administration, Atlanta, Ga.

4. "Providing Medical Evidence for individuals with AIDS and ARC," issued by the Social Security Administration, Miami Beach office.

5. See n. 1, *supra.*

6. *S.P. et al. v. Louis Sullivan, M.D., Secretary of the United States Department of Health and Human Services, S.D.N.Y., No. 90-CIV-6294-MGC.* See *AIDS Lit. Rptr.,* October 12, 1990, p. 5167.

7. "CDC Expands Definition of AIDS Cases," *The Miami Herald,* August 8, 1991, p. 23A.

4

Confidentiality

Issues of confidentiality are intricately intertwined with virtually all other issues touched by HIV disease. With genuine confidentiality, there would be a minimal, if any, opportunity for the kinds of discrimination that we have seen occurring against those who are or may be infected with HIV. With any chance for a lack of confidentiality, horror stories happen, and the possibility of them colors a subject's every thought and action.

First, one must understand the difference between confidentiality and anonymity. Confidential information is tied in some manner to some person who or entity that could later be identified as related to that information. The notion is that the party in possession of confidential information will keep the information itself or any manner of linking that information to its particular subject from passing or being passed along to others. With confidentiality, there is always the risk of breach and leak of the information or identity.

Anonymity, on the other hand, involves some manner of

information without any identification that could later tie the information to the individual subject of it. Even if the information were to pass from one possessor to another, the identity to whom or to which it might otherwise be linked is and remains by definition an unknown.

One case strikingly points out the difference between confidentiality and anonymity. It involved the names of some 350 persons who received confidential tests for HIV antibodies and venereal diseases. One medical laboratory sued another for money owed for performing the tests, and during the litigation, the names of the test subjects were inadvertently made public. Because the identities of the test subjects were confidential but not anonymous, the records contained those subjects' names, and the subjects' fears of leakage of their having taken the tests came true. Had the test result information been anonymous—that is, containing no identifying information—no embarrassment could have occurred. A senior attorney with the attorney general's office of the state in which this incident occurred commented that these were not really medical records and that release of the names was, therefore, not really a violation of the state's patient confidentiality laws.[1] I'm sure that was a great comfort to those whose medical histories had just been made the talk of their towns.

And practices in an area quite near where this litigation leak occurred point out all the more clearly the danger inherent in merely confidential information. Fire department officials in two cities admitted keeping one list of people they believed had AIDS and another list of addresses where someone with AIDS was suspected of living. The story in one of the cities came to light when a woman arrested for prostitution was subsequently charged with attempted murder after police were told by the town's fire department that her name appeared on a list of people with AIDS. The fire chief said that fire rescue workers had an informal, secret written list of people they believed had tested positive for HIV, with the list being for their private use. However, a sheriff's department spokesman later clarified that the woman had been tested about six months earlier, with negative results.[2]

Bail for the woman was then set at a minimal $10, with prosecutors expected to drop the charge.[3]

The other city with a "secret" list had a 911 computer system in the fire department that flashed "AIDS patient" when dealing with an address at which the computer system had been advised that an HIV-infected person lived.[4] One would have to consider oneself fortunate to have no enemies with access to that computer system.

Several other similar cases have arisen in the criminal law context. In Delaware in June 1990, the state attorney general rendered an opinion that maintenance of data about an individual's HIV status as a part of the state's criminal-records information system would constitute an improper and unwarranted intrusion into the individual's privacy.[5]

But in March 1990, a state court in New York declined to issue an order protecting the identity of a deceased defendant from disclosure by the plaintiff. The court saw the legislative intent for confidentiality as being to increase voluntary testing for HIV antibodies, not provision of protection for civil defendants and particularly not when weighed against the public policy of open court proceedings. The court said release of the identity would not prejudice the rights of a deceased party.[6]

Similarly, a federal court in Rhode Island denied a motion by survivors of one who had died of AIDS-related causes when those survivors sought to use pseudonyms in a suit against an insurer. The court said that an insufficient basis had been presented to overcome the presumption that court pleadings filed are public documents.[7]

And in a strange version of the criminal law issues, a federal court dismissed a breach of confidentiality suit filed by a federal corrections system inmate who complained that his having tested negative for HIV antibodies was unnecessarily disclosed to a prison official. The court called the suit "frivolous" and observed that the plaintiff was "clearly not within the group of persons protected" and had not even alleged any harm resulting from the disclosure.[8]

More than one doctor has been sued when the results of a patient's HIV-antibody test were inappropriately disclosed to third parties. In Florida, for example, where confidentiality of HIV-antibody test results is mandated by statute with only limited exceptions, suit was filed in 1988 against a physician who provided such test results to the subject patient's employer. The patient/employee, a surgical technician, was fired.[9]

And the right to privacy has been heavily relied on in these kinds of cases. In New Jersey, after police had already been alerted to "John Doe's" HIV-positive status by Doe himself as he was being searched by police in an earlier incident, Doe's neighbor was told of that infection status when Doe later was involved in a minor traffic incident. The neighbor allegedly then told the parents of other children who attended the same school as Doe's children and further told the media of Doe's condition. Reportedly, 19 children were removed from the school, and the family was ostracized in the community. Doe sued both the police officer who unnecessarily gave the information to the neighbor, the city for which that police officer worked, and the offending neighbor.[10] In January 1990, the court held that there is a constitutional right of privacy for people known to have or suspected of having AIDS, and it extended that right to members of the immediate family of the infected persons. Moreover, the court found that a municipality that had not trained its employees in the need for confidentiality of AIDS-related information can be held liable for the improper release of that information.[11]

Probably the largest number of these cases has arisen regarding transfusions or injections that are the alleged source of a plaintiff's HIV infection. One of the earliest cases on this issue occurred in Florida, which has a particularly strong, constitutional-level right-to-privacy provision. The state's supreme court used the case to establish all the more clearly the paramount importance of the right to privacy and denied access to blood-donor identities.[12]

And in late 1990, in a suit against the Red Cross by the recipient of alleged HIV-tainted blood for failure to adequately screen blood, the plaintiff's motion to compel discovery of the identity of the donor was denied. The court said that the potential danger to the volunteer blood-supply system far outweighed the individual plaintiff's need for the disclosure.[13]

In a California case in which the trial court had authorized anonymous depositions of blood donors, an appellate court held that even anonymous depositions would violate that state's law requiring privacy for blood donors. Even if allowed to testify from behind a screen, the donors would be seen or heard during the deposition by at least the referee and the court reporter.[14]

Other cases have not always been as solidly on the side of privacy, however. Also in late 1990, a New Jersey court ruled that the recipient of an alleged HIV-tainted blood transfusion would be permitted to question the donor (or review the donor's medical records if the donor were then dead) in order to determine whether there was negligence in the formulation and implementation of measures to provide safer blood once the manner of HIV transmission was understood.[15] The New Jersey Supreme Court has agreed to review the ruling.[16]

And in early 1991, the Oklahoma Supreme Court affirmed without comment a trial court's granting of a motion to disclose the donor whose blood the plaintiff in the case alleged had infected her with HIV.[17]

At about the same time, a trial court in South Carolina allowed questioning of a donor who apparently gave HIV-infected blood used in a transfusion for a premature infant. Saying that the information was "not only relevant, but crucial," the judge proposed to have a court-appointed intermediary submit written questions to the donor, whose identity was ordered to be provided in a sealed envelope. The judge said that the information sought did not invade the donor's privacy interest under that state's laws, and even if it did, the donor's interest was outweighed by the injured party's need for the information. As to one argument used successfully in other cases, the ruling included the observation that "there is not one shred of tangible evidence in the nature of hard statistical data to substantiate an otherwise speculative claim that the blood supply will be jeopardized."[18]

In what seems to be a mixed-result case, a California appellate court found that a right to privacy does arise "in the disclosure of HIV-positive status to a health-care worker for the purpose of alerting the worker to the need for taking safety precautions in handling medical implements contaminated with blood." Although the health-care worker may have rightfully had access to the information obtained during a physical exam for injuries that were received in an industrial accident, the court found that the supervising physician's having later told the patient's insurer was "improper use of information properly obtained."[19]

And in a move that many AIDS activists would applaud, the chief of the infectious diseases department at the University of Colorado Health Sciences Center, working on a project to try to find a cure for AIDS, refused to comply with a Colorado law that requires him to turn over to the state health department the names of patients taking part in work on experimental AIDS drugs and who test positive for HIV.[20]

Issues of confidentiality are dealt with again in a special context in Chapter 22, "The Right to Know," in which patients' right to know whether a medical service provider is HIV-positive is examined as well as medical service providers' right to know the same of patients.

NOTES

1. "Suit Names AIDS-Test Patients," an Associated Press story appearing in the *Fort Lauderdale Sun-Sentinel*, November 3, 1990, p. 29A.

2. "Two Florida City Fire Departments Keep, Share Lists of PWAs, Others 'Suspected' of Being HIV-Positive," *The Weekly News*, December 12, 1990, p. 3.

3. "Case Based on AIDS List Expected to Be Dropped," an Associated Press story appearing in *The Miami Herald*, December 9, 1990, p. 10C.

4. See n. 2, *supra*.

5. "AIDS Information in the DELJIS Data Base," DE Atty.

Gen. Opinion No. 90–I011. See *AIDS Lit. Rptr.*, June 22, 1990, p. 4695.

6. *Flynn v. Doe*, Sup. Ct., N.Y. Cty., N.Y.L.J., March 30, 1990, pp. 25–26. See *AIDS Update*, Lambda Legal Defense and Education Fund, Inc., Vol. 4, No. 2 (July 1990), p. 1.

7. *Doe v. Prudential Insurance Co. of America*, D.R.I., No. 90–0207–T. See *AIDS Lit. Rptr.*, October 26, 1990, p. 5246. The appeal of the denial of use of pseudonyms was later withdrawn so that the case could proceed. See *AIDS Lit. Rptr.*, November 9, 1990, p. 5335.

8. *Beasley v. Fountain*, D. Kan., No. 90–3519–S. See *AIDS Lit. Rptr.*, February 8, 1991, p. 5789.

9. *Kautz v. Orizonda*, FL Cir. Ct., 9th Jud. Cir. See *AIDS Update*, Lambda Legal Defense and Education Fund, Inc., Vol. 2, No. 6 (March 1988), p. 1.

10. *Doe v. Borough of Barrington*, D.N.J., C.A. No. 88–2642. See *AIDS Update*, Lambda Legal Defense and Education Fund, Inc., Vol. 3, No. 9 (July 1989), p. 1.

11. *Id.* See *AIDS Update*, Vol. 4, No. 1 (May 1990), p. 1.

12. *Rasmussen v. South Florida Blood Service*, 500 So.2d 533 (Fla. 1987).

13. *Coleman v. American Red Cross Blood Services, Southeastern Michigan Region*, 130 F.R.D. 360 (E.D. Mich. 1990). See *AIDS Update*, Lambda Legal Defense and Education Fund, Inc., Vol. 4, No. 2 (December 1990), p. 9.

14. *Irwin Memorial Blood Bank v. Superior Court of San Francisco County*, CA Ct. of App., 1st Dist., Div. 4, Nos. A051352, A052325. See *AIDS Lit. Rptr.*, April 26, 1991, p. 6165.

15. *Snyder v. Mekhjian*, NJ Super. Ct., App. Div., No. A–5446–89T1. See *AIDS Lit. Rptr.*, November 23, 1990, p. 5407.

16. *Ibid.*, NJ Sup. Ct., No. 32,876, M–532, September Term 1990. See *AIDS Lit. Rptr.*, March 8, 1991, p. 5924.

17. *Oklahoma Blood Institute v. Gullett*, OK Sup. Ct., No. 76,961, on appeal from *Spiegel v. Fisher*, OK Dist. Ct., Oklahoma Cty., No. CJ–88–7109. See *AIDS Lit. Rptr.*, March 22, 1991, p. 5999.

18. *Watson v. Medical University of South Carolina et al.*, D.S.C., Charleston Div., No. 88–2844–18, implementation stayed and issue certified, *Watson v. American National Red Cross*, 4th Cir., No. 91–2053. See *AIDS Lit. Rptr.*, June 14, 1991, p. 6383.

19. *Estate of Gary Urbaniak v. Newton et al.*, CA Ct. of App., 1st Dist., Div. 1, No. AO45593. See *AIDS Lit. Rptr.*, February 8,

1991, p. 5781. See also *AIDS Update,* Lambda Legal Defense and Education Fund, Inc., Vol. 4, No. 4 (March 1991), p. 8, citing as 277 Cal. Rptr. 354 (Cal. App. 1991).

20. "AIDS Study Is at Odds with Law," an Associated Press story appearing in the *Fort Lauderdale Sun-Sentinel,* January 13, 1991, p. 6A.

5

Consumer Fraud

Cynical though the statement may sound, it is a truism that every crisis brings forth those who seek to take advantage of others for their own economic benefit. Con artists prey on the weak, no matter what the source of that weakness, and the fear generated by the news that one is HIV-positive makes those infected with the virus easy targets.

State attorneys general and the Federal Trade Commission have already encountered multiple consumer frauds aimed at those with HIV infection. These schemes come and go, changing corporate identities, trade names, and locales at the drop of a hat. Therefore, we'll sample only a few in order to provide a bit of the flavor of what the PWA community faces in addition to medical and discrimination problems.

In April 1988, the Attorney General of Florida was sufficiently concerned about these issues that staff of his Consumer Litigation Section issued a call for people to turn in ads for products promising what medical science can't deliver or offering clearly fraudulent goods to the public. Already under investigation was the offer for sale of household disinfectant at as much as $20 per bottle to kill the AIDS virus on such places as telephones, toilet seats, and lunch counters, all places where the virus cannot live more than momentarily and from which transmission does not occur.[1]

In March 1989, AIDS officials expressed alarm at a former employee of a state AIDS program selling an alternative therapy, with some of the literature using the word "cure," for *only* $50,000. The purchase price included round-trip airfare to Zaire, where the treatment was discovered, a two-month stay in a villa, and the alternative therapy drug treatment. The entrepreneur's former supervisors expressed concern over the confidentiality of state records, including patients' identities. The U.S. Food and Drug Administration knew nothing of the drug being offered, and others within the international AIDS community strongly suggested that publication of research results would seem to be a more appropriate approach than selling the treatment package for that sizable sum.[2]

In October 1990, a south Florida newspaper exposed the sale for $7,500 of a device that it said could be built for $700 to $800 and that the promoter, whom the newspaper called a "convicted con man," claimed could help heal AIDS (and cancer, Alzheimer's disease, the flu, and other illnesses). The technique was supposedly "ozone therapy." Medical experts termed the claim ridiculous and said that the treatment could be dangerous if people used it and avoided conventional medical treatments or if they exposed themselves to dangerous or contaminated levels of ozone.[3]

The promoter of the ozone therapy device was indicted by a federal grand jury on ten counts of fraudulently persuading people with various illnesses, including AIDS, to buy the ozone machines for as much as $7,500. He had already been charged by state authorities with practicing medicine without a license.[4]

Similarly, Dallas-based International White Cross was enjoined by a federal court, at the request of the Federal Trade Commission (FTC), from claiming that its nutritional supplement product, "Immune Plus," or any similar products will cure AIDS or that the products' effectiveness has been shown by scientifically valid clinical studies. According to the FTC, ads for that product "would lead anyone to believe this is a cure for AIDS."[5]

In June 1991, a Virginia laboratory director who used vitamins, herbs, and other unconventional methods to treat people with AIDS withdrew his application for a medical license. He did so ten months after being convicted of practicing medicine without a license.[6]

And two Scottsdale, Arizona, men were charged with six counts of felony fraud in April 1991 for allegedly selling health insurance that would cover policyholders who contracted AIDS. Undercover investigators posed as potential customers and were asked for saliva samples to test for HIV antibodies. As of this writing, saliva is not a valid test for HIV antibodies. Moreover, neither of the men charged were even licensed to sell insurance in Arizona.[7]

Saying that it would "not tolerate this type of illegal short circuiting of the system, particularly with regard to products for serious diseases like AIDS," the U.S. Food and Drug Administration (FDA) announced in July 1991 that two firms had agreed to stop marketing a saliva-based kit that allegedly tested for HIV antibodies. The kits did not have FDA approval but were being used by insurance companies to screen applicants.[8]

Also in July 1991, the Minnesota Attorney General sued a businessman who said he could help clients find out if their medical practitioners were HIV-positive. The entrepreneur advertised that his "legally prepared, lifesaving" forms could be used to determine HIV status of health-care workers—and for a cost of just $22.95. Calling the promises "fraud in its darkest form," the attorney general said that the papers were "nothing more than a sham and have no significance whatsoever." The same businessman had reportedly been sued by the state attorney general in 1975 for turning back odometers on used cars that he sold.[9]

Even "Dear Abby" has gotten in on the push to ensure that these companies don't prey successfully on those whose judgment may be clouded by fear and desperation. Commenting on an advertisement for a "specially treated towelette that will destroy the AIDS virus!," she wisely cautioned that one should call the nearest AIDS hotline or the local public health department for information on any such new miracle product before sending for anything that makes such promises.[10]

NOTES

1. "State Targets AIDS Fraud in Advertising," *Palm Beach Post,* April 10, 1988, p. 16D.

2. "'Cure' Alarms AIDS Officials," *The Miami Herald,* March 28, 1989, p. 1A.

3. "Ozone Device Dangerous, Engineers Say," *Fort Lauderdale Sun-Sentinel,* October 7, 1990, p. 3B.

4. "Federal Grand Jury Indicts Wainwright in Ozone Treatments," *Fort Lauderdale Sun-Sentinel,* April 4, 1991, p. 1B.

5. *Federal Trade Commission v. International White Cross et al.,* N.D. Cal., No. C91-0377TEH. See *AIDS Lit. Rptr.,* April 12, 1991, p. 6094, and "Judge Bans Ads Touting Nutrition Supplement as AIDS Cure," *The Weekly News,* March 13, 1991, p. 34.

6. *The Advocate,* No. 582 (July 30, 1991), p. 30.

7. *The Advocate,* No. 576 (May 7, 1991), p. 36.

8. *The Advocate,* No. 583 (August 13, 1991), p. 22.

9. *The Advocate,* No. 584 (August 27, 1991), p. 27.

10. "Shysters Capitalizing on the Fear of AIDS," a syndicated "Dear Abby" column appearing in the *Fort Lauderdale Sun-Sentinel,* March 23, 1988, p. 2E.

6

Criminal Law

As one might expect, HIV disease has had a great deal of interplay with the criminal law. The interplay arose from the nature of the groups in which HIV disease initially surfaced with prevalence—intravenous drug users, prostitutes, and homosexuals—as well as the relationships that those groups and others have with the criminal justice and prison systems, whether or not we like or agree with those relationships.

In looking at the various cases that have arisen in this context, let us try to do so in the order that the subtopics might occur, with our examination looking first at the various kinds of charges leveled against those with HIV disease.

Several cases have involved actual homicide charges of varying degrees. An Indiana case provided the setting for the first homicide-related conviction of this kind in the United States. The defendant had attempted to spray his blood on emergency medical service personnel who had arrived at the defendant's home and spoiled the defendant's suicide attempt. The judge, however, overturned the jury

conviction on those charges and reduced the offense to battery. It was the first time in the judge's 20-year tenure that
he had reversed a jury finding.[1]

In Florida, attempted manslaughter charges were
brought against a woman who agreed to engage in sexual
intercourse but failed to tell her sexual partner that she
knew she was HIV-positive.[2] The court granted a motion to
dismiss those charges, saying that although the defendant
"may have certainly acted in a culpably negligent fashion
. . . there is no evidence from which a jury could find that
her alleged conduct evidenced an intent to kill," which was
required for conviction of that charge under state law.
Charges of engaging in prostitution while infected with HIV
remained.[3]

And a New Jersey inmate was convicted of attempted
murder after biting a sheriff's officer and yelling, "Now die,
you pig; die from what I have." Not much question there
about demonstrating the requisite intent. The inmate was
sentenced to 25 years for the biting and for an accompanying assault charge involving another guard during the same
confrontation.[4]

Another case in which second degree murder charges resulted in a conviction occurred in California. In July 1991,
the state supreme court refused to reconsider the case of a
San Diego man who helped an HIV-positive acquaintance
strangle himself. The defendant had asserted that his friend
was despondent over his HIV status.[5]

Assault with a dangerous or deadly weapon seems to be a
charge with which a substantial number of HIV-infected defendants have been charged. One of the first cases was
against an HIV-positive federal inmate in Minnesota who
was found guilty of such charges for having bitten two correctional officers during a scuffle.[6]

In what is believed to be the first charges of assault with
a deadly weapon arising from alleged knowing transmission
of the virus sexually, an HIV-positive defendant in the District of Columbia was convicted of 26 sexual violations, including sodomy, indecent acts on a minor, and enticing a minor. The assault with a deadly weapon charges were

dropped, however, as prosecutors failed to show that the defendant had actually transmitted the virus to anyone.[7]

The first reported case in California of charges of assault with a deadly weapon for sexual transmission involved an HIV-positive man who continued to have unprotected sex with a woman after he knew of his infection and had been warned that failure to use a condom could risk infecting a partner. He was indicted on 15 counts for repeatedly exposing and infecting the woman with HIV, where both the woman and a child that she claimed the defendant fathered tested positive for HIV.[8]

And a man who allegedly had sex with a female acquaintance at least four times without telling her that he was HIV-positive reportedly once boasted that he would "take all the women I can with me before I die," according to the case's prosecutor. The defendant was charged with assault with a deadly weapon in April 1991, with the assistant district attorney handling the case saying that the defendant had set out to "ritually infect sex partners out of spite."[9]

Somewhat similarly, in late 1989, an HIV-positive man was convicted of assault with a deadly weapon for biting a police officer who answered a domestic quarrel disturbance call. This case was unusual in that the court articulated reasoning that the teeth of a PWA are akin to a boxer's "killer's hands."[10] The conviction was upheld by the Georgia Court of Appeals, saying that what mattered was not whether saliva could constitute a deadly weapon but rather the defendant's intent, with that intent having been demonstrated during the proceedings of the case by testimony that the defendant sucked up saliva before biting into the officer's arm.[11]

A Texas grand jury indicted a man in June 1991 on charges of trying to expose a police officer to HIV by spitting. The man was accused of biting his lip and spitting blood on officers while running from the scene of an accident. Prosecutors alleged that the defendant had told one of the officers he had AIDS and was going to expose her; the defense asserted that the defendant was HIV-negative and lied about his status because he was angry.[12]

And a Kansas man was charged in July 1991 with aggra-

vated assault for scratching and spitting on three law enforcement officers after telling them he was HIV-positive.
Bond was set at $75,000.[13]

The biting cases draw an inordinate amount of attention
considering what experts say is the minimal, if any, risk of
virus transmission by biting. An HIV-positive transsexual
who was originally arrested in Florida for drunken driving
was charged additionally with two counts of aggravated battery on correctional officers and one count of criminal mis-
chief for allegedly biting two female police officers. The trial
included testimony from the director of the state health department's AIDS Program that "AIDS cannot be transmitted
by biting, and therefore [biting] cannot be a deadly
weapon." "There have been 146,000 cases of AIDS reported,
and there has been no report of AIDS transmission by biting.
From what we know it is not transmittable by biting," he
testified. Nevertheless, the defendant was convicted and
sentenced to six years in prison.[14]

Probably the strangest of the assault-with-a-deadly-
weapon cases is that of an HIV-positive man who forced his
blood-covered hand across the mouth of his live-in girlfriend
during a domestic dispute. The jury deadlocked in an eight-
to-four vote, and the prosecutor indicated that retrial would
not be sought in light of the conviction of the defendant on
accompanying charges of spousal abuse.[15]

The next group of charges involves knowing exposure of
another person to the virus. These charges are generally less
than assault with a deadly weapon and are, in most cases,
brought under statutes enacted as a result of the HIV epidemic. What were believed to have been the first such
charges in Idaho were dropped when the defendant was imprisoned on other charges, including lewd and lascivious
conduct with a minor.[16]

A former Boise State University basketball player was
shortly thereafter charged with four felony counts of knowingly transmitting HIV-infected bodily fluids and two counts
of statutory rape and was held on $1 million bond.[17] He sub-
sequently pleaded guilty to a single rape charge in exchange
for having the remaining counts dropped just days before

the scheduled start of his trial[18] and was sentenced to three to 15 years in prison.[19]

In Washington state, a 30-year-old man was the first to be charged with failing to inform a sexual partner of HIV infection, a second-degree misdemeanor under that state's law. He was given a maximum jail term of ten years.[20]

California's "knowing exposure" law includes a special provision applicable to those already convicted of prostitution and who have tested HIV-positive. In 1990, a 29-year-old man became the first in Los Angeles to be charged under that provision, the charges stemming from his allegedly having solicited an undercover police officer for sex.[21] The felony prostitution charge was dropped, with the municipal court saying that he was not properly warned that he could be charged with a felony if he were arrested again for prostitution.[22] That charge was reinstated, however, when the decision was overturned on appeal to the state superior court, and an appellate court refused to disturb that reinstatement of the charge.[23]

In Illinois, a 34-year-old man who had repeatedly tested HIV-positive was convicted of aggravated criminal assault for knowingly exposing his eight-year-old adoptive brother to HIV by having ejaculated into the brother's mouth while they shared a bed, thus becoming the apparent first conviction under that state's "knowing exposure" law.[24]

And an Ohio defendant was sentenced to the maximum of life in prison for murdering a woman who said to him, "Welcome to the world of AIDS," after the pair had met in a bar and had sex in her car. The defendant then reportedly beat her and torched her car with her body still inside. The prosecution argued that the defendant had invented the story in an attempt to justify the killing; any use of the story as a defense was undermined by the defendant's admission that he continued to wear jeans soaked with the victim's blood for some time after the killing.[25]

Illinois police were reported to be stepping up enforcement of a state law that makes it a felony for HIV-positive people to engage in high-risk sex, with charges filed in June 1991 against two suspected prostitutes.[26]

And a Missouri man was sentenced to three years in prison in that same month for failing to tell his gay lover that he had AIDS, according to one of the nation's leading gay news magazines. The prosecution was believed to have been the first under that state's law that requires people with AIDS to disclose their medical condition to sexual partners.[27]

According to the director of the AIDS Litigation Project of the U.S. Public Health Service, a professor at the Harvard University School of Public Health, 22 states passed laws from 1986 to 1990 making illegal conduct that could transmit HIV.[28] He noted that most of the successful prosecutions had involved military personnel, with most civilian cases involving biting, spitting, or splashing blood rather than intercourse and that "[i]t is virtually impossible—if not impossible—to transmit the virus that way. It appears . . . to be much more punitive than effectuating any clear public policy," he said.[29]

A different kind of knowing exposure case arose when a Tennessee woman called for emergency medical assistance because her fiancé had suffered a heart attack. Police and ambulance attendants coming to the man's aid gave him mouth-to-mouth resuscitation and other emergency assistance, according to the judge. For failing to tell the would-be rescuers that the patient was HIV-positive, the woman was charged with reckless endangerment, a felony punishable by up to six years in prison.[30]

Several other kinds of criminal charges have also been lodged in connection with HIV disease. In 1988, a California jury acquitted a mentally ill man charged with attempted poisoning after he tried to sell his HIV-positive blood to a plasma center. Other charges of attempted murder and assault had already been dismissed by the judge. Apparently, the jury agreed with the defense that the man had only the intent to get the money that the blood sale would generate rather than the degree of intent required for the poisoning charge.[31]

An HIV-positive Washington state man was convicted of exploitation for paying to take Polaroid photographs of a 16-year-old boy and patronizing a juvenile prostitute by offering to pay him money.[32]

An Iowa man was acquitted of charges that he set fire to the AIDS hospice where he lived. It was alleged that he had set the fire to collect the insurance money on possessions he kept stored in the hospice's garage.[33]

A Harvard University student was arrested on suspicion of trying to blackmail a physician who tested positive for HIV antibodies by threatening to expose him to the news media and the American Medical Association if the doctor did not pay $10,000. The student was working during the summer break in Los Angeles, where the charges were brought.[34]

And there has even been one case of criminal charges for AIDS-related discrimination. Based on a local ordinance, the city of West Hollywood, California, filed criminal charges against the proprietor of a nail salon who refused to serve a PWA.[35] A pedicurist and the salon's manager were later added as defendants.[36]

There have also been several marijuana-related cases involving persons with HIV disease. In mid-1990, a Florida court denied claims that a couple's use of marijuana was medically necessary to counteract the nausea and other side effects of the AIDS treatment drug AZT.[37] On appeal, the couple was found not guilty of the felony charge of growing marijuana. The implication from the ruling marks the first time that a U.S. court has found marijuana to be a medical necessity for AIDS.[38]

The Food and Drug Administration approved use of marijuana by an unidentified Veterans Administration patient believed to be one of less than three dozen for whom use has been approved for compassionate purposes since 1976. Assisted by the Alliance for Cannabis Therapeutics, the president of which is a glaucoma patient, the petition was believed to have been the first to win FDA approval in this regard.[39]

Some 44% of the 1,000 cancer specialists who responded to a 1990 Harvard University survey said that they tell their patients to use marijuana to control nausea from chemotherapy, with one leading oncologist who treats many people with AIDS saying that marijuana has an "important place in the practice of medicine."[40]

In April 1991, a three-judge panel of a federal appeals court expressed concern that the Drug Enforcement Agency may be using inappropriate criteria in determining that marijuana has no legitimate medical use and told the agency to restudy its opposition to the drug's therapeutic use.[41]

Hypodermic needles, too, have been the subject of AIDS-related criminal charges. In June 1991, a judge acquitted eight AIDS activists who operated a hypodermic needle exchange as a way to fight AIDS in a drug-infested area of New York City. The defendants ranged from young, recovering addicts to a 67-year-old nurse who were affiliated with the AIDS direct action group ACT-UP.[42] The judge ruled that the harm they may have caused was offset by the harm they sought to prevent, saying that health officials have not adequately responded to the AIDS crisis and the needle exchange was "necessary as an emergency measure to avert imminent public injury."[43]

Less than two weeks later, the National Commission on AIDS issued a report saying that the Bush administration uses a "myopic criminal-justice approach" that emphasizes punishment but neglects treatment that could inhibit the spread of HIV. The report called laws restricting sterile injection equipment "obsolete and dangerous to the public health," with one commission member saying that such laws "do not prevent drug abuse but . . . do increase HIV transmission." The commission recommended repeal of all laws restricting access to clean needles.[44]

One case has focused on a defendant's interest in being released on bail as the case against that defendant winds its way through the criminal justice system. A New York appellate court held in 1987 that it was an abuse of discretion to impose that the defendant test negative for HIV antibodies as a condition for release on bail. It was simply not a part of the statutory criteria for bail, the court said.[45]

And bail was the focus of another situation when a pregnant, HIV-infected prostitute—as one newspaper called her, a "veteran Fort Lauderdale hooker carrying the AIDS virus and a soon-to-be-born baby"[46]—had bond set at $100,000 by a judge who said she wanted to protect the defendant, her baby, and the public from AIDS.[47]

A new question arose in 1991 in an Arizona case in which the defendant had entered a guilty plea, then learned he was HIV-positive and was shortly thereafter sentenced to seven and one-half years in jail. Apparently, he attempted to withdraw his guilty plea after learning of his HIV-infection but was not allowed to do so. An appellate court reversed that ruling, saying that refusing to allow the change of plea after he learned that he would probably not outlive his sentence would be "manifestly unjust."[48]

Jury prejudice has also come under scrutiny as a factor in cases in which HIV disease is involved. In 1989, the Maryland Court of Appeals reversed a murder conviction, holding that in the absence of a sound reason for doing so, the wearing of gloves by court officers who feared contracting AIDS from the defendant unfairly prejudiced the jury against that defendant.[49] The gloves were worn on the basis of rumors from an unidentified source that the defendant had AIDS, and the judge failed to conduct an investigation to determine whether there was any reason for the gloves.

The Maryland decision is in accord with a recommendation of the American Bar Association (ABA) that a criminal prosecution involving a defendant known or perceived to be infected with HIV proceed in the same fashion as any other case. "No unusual safety or security precautions should be employed, unless the defendant is violent or poses a demonstrated risk of escape," said the ABA.[50]

Any number of cases have involved requests for leniency because of a criminal defendant's HIV disease. Sampling just a few, a New York court in 1990 granted a defendant's motion to dismiss drug sale and possession charges against him because of the critical stage of his AIDS illness and medical estimates that he had less than six months to live. The court noted that the offense charged was "serious, but not violent or unusual" and "caused no harm to any specific person" in addition to the case meeting the other criteria usually used to determine eligibility for hardship dismissal of criminal charges.[51]

As 1990 turned to 1991, New York Governor Mario Cuomo granted clemency to a 35-year-old inmate dying of AIDS, the first time that the governor had cited the disease as a factor in granting a prisoner's request for a chance at freedom.[52]

Also in New York, charges of criminal sale of a controlled substance and criminal possession of a hypodermic instrument against an asymptomatic HIV-positive homeless man were dropped in 1991 in a case in which the judge rejected other courts' distinctions of defendants who had progressed to full AIDS.[53]

And again in New York, charges of grand larceny and possession of stolen property were dismissed against an HIV-infected defendant based on evidence that he was about to succumb to AIDS.[54] Testimony indicated that his life expectancy was only four to six months, and the court criticized prosecutors for suggesting that the defendant would receive better medical treatment if forced to remain incarcerated.

But in New Jersey in 1990, an appellate court noted that there was "no basis to create a special class of defendants entitled to lesser penalties" simply because they may be infected with HIV or have AIDS and, thus, upheld the sentence against the defendant without special consideration of his medical condition as a mitigating factor.[55]

And finally, in the criminal law process comes sentencing, with several cases being noteworthy. An Idaho defendant was sentenced to life imprisonment without the possibility of parole for having had sex with a 15-year-old boy.[56] And the defendant in the Polaroid photo exploitation case was given a sentence of seven and one-half years, double the usual 45 months, with that sentence having been upheld by the Washington State Supreme Court.[57] Both defendants felt that prejudice against persons with HIV disease and prejudice against gays were factors that worked toward the particularly harsh sentences.

NOTES

1. *Indiana v. Haines*, IN Super. Ct., Tippicanoe Cty., No. S–5585, February 25, 1988. See *AIDS Update*, Lambda Legal Defense and Education Fund, Inc., Vol. 2, No. 7 (April 1988), p. 2.

2. *State of Florida v. Sherouse,* FL Cir. Ct., Orange Cty., No. 87–7057, filed December 17, 1987, amended January 15, 1988. See *AIDS Update,* Lambda Legal Defense and Education Fund, Inc., Vol. 2, No. 6 (March 1988), p. 1.

3. *Id.* See *AIDS Update,* Lambda Legal Defense and Education Fund, Inc., Vol. 2, No. 7 (April 1988), p. 1.

4. *State of New Jersey v. Smith,* NJ Super. Ct., Camden Cty., Nos. 2114-8-89, I-2890-11-89. See *AIDS Lit. Rptr.,* June 8, 1990, p. 4604.

5. *The Advocate,* No. 584 (August 27, 1991), p. 26.

6. *U.S. v. Moore,* D. Minn., Crim. No. 4-87-44. See *AIDS Update,* Lambda Legal Defense and Education Fund, Inc., Vol. 2, No. 2 (August 1987), p. 2.

7. *District of Columbia v. Feaster,* DC Super. Ct., No. F3313-89. See *AIDS Lit. Rptr.,* August 10, 1990, p. 4908.

8. *California v. Crother,* CA Super. Ct., Ventura Cty., No. CR 27427. See *AIDS Lit. Rptr.,* February 22, 1991, p. 5850, as well as "Man Charged in Infection of Mom, Baby with AIDS," a Los Angeles Times Service story appearing in *The Miami Herald,* January 13, 1991, p. 11A.

9. "Prosecutor: Man Vowed to Give Women AIDS," *The Miami Herald,* April 14, 1991, p. 9A.

10. *Georgia v. Scroggins,* GA Super. Ct., Cobb Cty., No. 89-1288. See *AIDS Lit. Rptr.,* November 24, 1989, p. 3634.

11. *Scroggins v. State of Georgia,* GA Ct. of App., No. A90A1140, -41, -42, -44. See *AIDS Lit. Rptr.,* November 23, 1990, p. 5405.

12. *The Advocate,* No. 582 (July 22, 1991), p. 30.

13. *The Advocate,* No. 583 (August 13, 1991), p. 23.

14. "Judge Hands HIV-Positive Transsexual Six-Year Jail Term for Biting Guards; Lawyer Charges Harassment," *The Weekly News,* December 26, 1990, p. 10.

15. *People of the State of California v. Provost,* CA Super. Ct., Shasta Cty., No. 90-7393. See *AIDS Lit. Rptr.,* January 11, 1991, p. 5626.

16. See *AIDS Lit. Rptr.,* June 8, 1990, p. 4608.

17. *Ada County v. Thomas,* ID Dis. Ct., 4th Dist., Ada Cty., No. M9002909. See *AIDS Lit. Rptr.,* June 8, 1990, p. 4608.

18. *Id.* See *AIDS Lit. Rptr.,* September 28, 1990, p. 5100.

19. *Id.* See *AIDS Lit. Rptr.,* December 14, 1990, p. 5487.

20. *State of Washington v. Stark,* WA Super. Ct., Clallan Cty., No. 90-1-00030-2. See *AIDS Lit. Rptr.,* July 13, 1990, p. 4746.

21. *People v. Santangelo*, Los Angeles Municipal Ct., No. BA 027006. See *AIDS Lit. Rptr.*, October 26, 1990, p. 5256.

22. "AIDS Case Dismissed," *Fort Lauderdale Sun-Sentinel*, October 26, 1990, p. 3A.

23. *People v. Santangelo*, CA Ct. of App., 2nd Dist. See *AIDS Lit. Rptr.*, March 22, 1991, p. 6001.

24. *People of the State of Illinois v. Dempsey*, IL Cir. Ct., Williamson Cty., No. 90–CF–147. See *AIDS Lit. Rptr.*, November 9, 1990, p. 5334. See also "AIDS Carrier on Trial in Child's Sex Assault," *The Miami Herald*, October 13, 1990, p. A2.

25. *State of Ohio v. Hengehold*, OH Cmmn. Pleas Ct., Hamilton Cty., No. B–905998. See *AIDS Lit. Rptr.*, February 8, 1991, p. 5784.

26. *The Advocate*, No. 582 (July 30, 1991), p. 29.

27. *The Advocate*, No. 583 (August 13, 1991), p. 23.

28. "22 States Have AIDS Assault Law," an Associated Press story appearing in the *Fort Lauderdale Sun-Sentinel*, October 22, 1990, p. 3A.

29. *Id.*

30. "Aid to Infected Man Leads to Criminal Charge," *The Miami Herald*, June 2, 1991, p. 11A.

31. *California v. Markowski*, CA Super. Ct., Los Angeles Cty., No. A954578. See *AIDS Update*, Lambda Legal Defense and Education Fund, Inc., Vol. 2, No. 8 (May 1988), p. 1.

32. "Appeals Court Upholds 'Extremely Harsh' Jail Term for Gay PWA," *The Weekly News*, March 20, 1991, p. 15.

33. *The Advocate*, No. 581 (July 16, 1991), p. 33.

34. "Student Held in AIDS Blackmail Plot," a Reuters story appearing in the *Fort Lauderdale Sun-Sentinel*, August 17, 1991, p. 9A.

35. *People v. Vartoughian et al.*, Municipal Ct., Beverly Hills, Los Angeles Cty., CA, No. M89613. See *AIDS Update*, Lambda Legal Defense and Education Fund, Inc., No. 14 (January 1987), p. 5. See also the companion civil case, *Jasperson v. Jessica's Nail Salon*. CA Super. Ct., Los Angeles Cty., No. B027279.

36. *Id.* See *AIDS Update*, Lambda Legal Defense and Education Fund, Inc., Vol. 2, No. 1 (June/July, 1987), p. 7.

37. *State of Florida v. Jenks*, FL Cir. Ct., Bay Cty., No. 90–0751. See *AIDS Lit. Rptr.*, August 24, 1990, p. 4954.

38. *Jenks v. Florida*, FL Ct. of App., 1st Dist., No. 90–2462. See *AIDS Lit. Rptr.*, April 26, 1991, p. 6166, and "Paralyzed Man, AIDS Couple Allowed Legal Use of Marijuana," a Reuters story

appearing in the *Fort Lauderdale Sun-Sentinel,* April 18, 1991, p. 16A.

39. "FDA Approves Marijuana for AIDS Patient," an Associated Press story appearing in the *Fort Lauderdale Sun-Sentinel,* November 23, 1990, p. 10A.

40. "Many Decry Shift On Marijuana Use As AIDS Treatment," *The Advocate,* No. 582 (July 30, 1991), p. 26.

41. "Court Orders DEA to Restudy Marijuana's Medical Value," an Associated Press story appearing in the *Fort Lauderdale Sun-Sentinel,* April 27, 1991, p. 18A.

42. *People of New York v. Bordowitz et al.,* New York City Crim. Ct., Jury 5, Nos. 90N028423–90N028426. See *AIDS Lit. Rptr.,* July 12, 1991, p. 6522.

43. "Needle Exchange OK," *USA Today,* June 26, 1991, p. 3A.

44. "Needle Exchanges Get Endorsement From AIDS Panel," *The Advocate,* No. 585 (September 10, 1991), p. 15.

45. *People v. McGreevy,* 514 N.Y.S.2d 622 (1987).

46. "Infected Hooker's Bond: $100,000," *The Miami Herald,* July 26, 1991, p. 1A.

47. *Id.*

48. *The Advocate,* No. 577 (May 21, 1991), p. 26.

49. *Wiggins v. Maryland,* 315 Md. 232, 554 A.2d 356 (1989).

50. "Policy on AIDS and the Criminal Justice System," adopted by the American Bar Association House of Delegates, February 7, 1989.

51. *People of New York v. Roman,* NY Sup. Ct., Bronx Cty., Criminal Term, Part 46, N.Y.L.J., October 5, 1990, p. 25. See *AIDS Lit. Rptr.,* October 26, 1990, p. 5255.

52. *The Miami Herald,* January 2, 1991, p. 2A.

53. *People of New York v. Suarez,* NY Sup. Ct., NY Cty., Criminal Term, Part 81, Indictment No. 5874-90. See *AIDS Lit. Rptr.,* March 8, 1991, p. 5925.

54. *People v. Jimmie E.,* NY Sup. Ct., NY Cty., IA Part 53. See *AIDS Lit. Rptr.,* April 26, 1991, p. 6170.

55. *New Jersey v. Bilella,* NJ Super. Ct., App. Div., No. A-5635-87T4. See *AIDS Lit. Rptr.,* May 11, 1990, p. 4462.

56. See n. 32.

57. *Id.*

7

Education

The single element of American society about which we are most protective is our children. Some combination of instinct and a recognition that children are unable to protect themselves has led to some reasonable and some rather bizarre protective measures by society, and the advent of AIDS has surely produced some particularly unusual protective measures regarding children.

Early on, the circle-the-wagons mentality surfaced in this area as well. In Michigan, a substitute teacher with AIDS was dismissed by the Board of Ann Arbor Public Schools. The case was ultimately settled in 1986 with the teacher receiving back pay and $10,000 in damages as well as attorneys' fees and a specific number of days for substitute teaching. What was significant about the case, though, was that even in that early time frame, the deputy director of the Michigan Department of Civil Rights suggested in a letter to the school board that, in his opinion, the board's policy of excluding people with AIDS violated the state's civil rights law.[1]

At about the same time, the Equal Rights Division of the Wisconsin Department of Industrial, Labor, and Human Relations ruled that the Racine school district's policy of prohibiting students and staff with AIDS or ARC from attending school violated the state's antidiscrimination laws. Noteworthy about this incident was that there had been as of then no reported cases of AIDS or ARC among students or faculty. When asked what criteria would be used to determine if a person has AIDS, a school board official replied that "the Rock Hudson look would be one of the primary characteristics."[2]

In Indiana, 13-year-old Ryan White endured education via telephone hookup between his bedroom and the classroom as he sued under the Federal Education for All Handicapped Children Act for the right to attend classes in person.[3] In New York, a courageous school board adopted a policy allowing students with AIDS to attend classes, but parents in Queens kept their children away from at least two schools in protest.[4]

It was not until November 1986 that a federal court finally ruled for the first time that AIDS is a handicap within the intent of the 1973 Rehabilitation Act, in that case allowing a five-year-old California youngster to return to school.[5] Other states acted guardedly through their administrative processes or only under court order in dealing with questions of their educational systems and AIDS.

In May 1987, the highest court in New Jersey upheld regulations requiring admission of children with AIDS or ARC to public schools, unless the child is not toilet-trained or is incontinent, unable to control drooling, or is unusually aggressive with a documented history of biting or harming others.[6]

In Florida, it took a court ruling in August 1987 before officials would allow the "Haitian triplets," as they were known, all of whom were infected with HIV, to attend a special program for handicapped children. Even then, only two of the three children survived long enough to enroll.[7] Also in Florida, a six-year-old who had been restricted to homebound education sued, alleging discrimination in that "homebound" was not the statutorily required "least restrictive alternative." A federal judge allowed her in school, but only if she would remain in an isolation booth because of her AIDS-related disabilities, including the lack of toilet self-sufficiency. That restriction was overturned by the U.S. Court of Appeals,[8] and the lower court then allowed the child into mainstream classrooms.[9]

Probably the best known of the Florida education cases is that of the Ray boys from Arcadia. Three sons of the Ray family in that small, rural community had all contracted HIV disease through treatments for hemophilia. When knowledge of their infection surfaced, the boys were barred from school (and the family barred from its church, and so on, in one of the nation's worst examples of the circle-the-wagons mentality). In a comparatively enlightened and early decision on this issue, a federal judge ruled that there was no reason to bar the boys from school and ordered them admitted.[10] Before the Ray boys could return to school, however, their home in Arcadia was burned in what was termed a "fire-bombing."

Perhaps the most significant of the school cases involved a California teacher named Chalk. A PWA, Mr. Chalk taught children with learning disabilities and was well-respected by the students, the parents, and apparently even by the members of the school board. Perhaps out of fear of suit by concerned parents, the local school board removed Chalk from the classroom, but it did so expecting him to contest the board's ruling and perhaps even hoping he would win. The ultimate decision came from the U.S. Court of Appeals, which ordered Chalk reassigned from his desk job back into the classroom.[11] With that decision, a court at the level just below the Supreme Court of the United States had ruled on the issue in a case not involving particularly unique circumstances, and the law on this issue was deemed well-established.

At this point, the rights of both HIV-infected students to be able to attend public schools and of HIV-infected teachers to be able to remain at the heads of their classes seem to be secure.

However, protective as our society is about its children,

variations of these and new, as yet unimagined issues will surely arise. And resistant as some segments of our society are to logic and reason, these issues will surely have to be litigated.

One such case involves parents belonging to a conservative religious organization seeking exemption of their children from a mandatory AIDS curriculum. A New York appellate court overturned a trial court's dismissal of the case, saying that there should have been a determination of whether the offered alternative education would meet the children's informational needs.[12]

In another instance, an AIDS education consultant's scheduled presentation to high school students was barred on the eve of the workshop when a poll of school board members found only one favoring letting the consultant speak.[13]

The American Bar Association has made specific recommendations in accord with the law as it has generally been shaped by these decisions. Among the recommendations:

- A student should not be excluded from school because of known or perceived HIV status;
- A student should not be separated from classmates because of known or perceived HIV status, except under specific circumstances in which the student's behavior risks transmission of the virus, efforts at counseling and training have not been or cannot be expected to be successful, and the manner of separation chosen is the least restrictive means of reducing the risk of transmission; and
- School authorities should afford maximum confidentiality to a student's HIV status.[14]

What new twists to education issues and AIDS will come next, we'll just have to wait and see.

NOTES

1. See *AIDS Update,* Lambda Legal Defense and Education Fund, Inc., No. 7 (June 1986), p. 8.

2. *Ibid.,* pp. 8–9.

3. *White v. Western School Corp.,* 1P 85–1192C (S.D. Ind. August 16, 1985).

4. See, for example, *District 27 Community School Bd. v. Board of Educ.,* 130 Misc. 398, 502 N.Y.S.2d 325 (1986).

5. *Thomas v. Atascadero Unified School Dist.,* 662 F.Supp. 376 (C.D. Cal. 1987).

6. See, for example, *Board of Educ. of Plainfield v. Cooperman,* 105 N.J. 587, 523 A.2d 655 (N.J. 1987).

7. *C.C. & his Minor Children v. Dade County School Board and United Teachers of Dade,* S.D. Fla., No. 86–1513–CIV–DAVIS. See also *AIDS Update,* Lambda Legal Defense and Education Fund, Inc., Vol. 2, No. 2 (August 1987), pp. 2–3.

8. *Martinez v. School Board of Hillsborough County, Florida,* 692 F.Supp. 1293 (M.D. Fla. 1988), rev'd. 861 F.2d 1502 (11th Cir. 1988).

9. *Martinez v. School Board of Hillsborough County, Florida,* 711 F.Supp. 1066 (M.D. Fla. 1989).

10. *Ray v. School Dist. of DeSoto County,* 666 F.Supp. 1524 (M.D. Fla. 1987).

11. *Chalk v. United States District Court of Cal.,* 840 F.2d 701 (9th Cir. 1988).

12. *Ware v. Valley Stream School District,* N.Y. Ct. App., No. 292, December 19, 1989. See *AIDS Update,* Vol. 4, No. 1 (May 1990), p. 3.

13. "School Board Halts AIDS Workshop," an Associated Press story appearing in *The Weekly News,* October 24, 1990, p. 8.

14. "Policy on AIDS," adopted by the House of Delegates of the American Bar Association, August 1989, p. 8.

8

Employment

We should begin this discussion by recalling that the Rehabilitation Act of 1973, the most pertinent portion of which is generally known as "Section 504,"[1] prohibits discrimination on the basis of handicap against any otherwise qualified individual in any program or activity that receives federal financial assistance. This law, which surely predated by almost a decade the issues specifically associated with HIV disease, is why we have seen special facilities for the handicapped on college campuses, in state and local government office buildings, in hospitals, and wherever government dollars are involved.

Next, we need to recognize that many civil rights laws are generally enforced and administered by the U.S. Department of Justice. Section 504, however, is generally administered by the U.S. Department of Health and Human Services (HHS). Even so, Justice serves a role to HHS much as an attorney would serve to a client—though HHS has its own in-department legal counsel, HHS can and did ask Justice for a formal legal opinion on issues affected by the laws it administers.

In this instance, HHS came to Justice and asked about the enforcement of Section 504 relative to AIDS issues: specifically, was the employment of HIV-infected persons covered by the antidiscrimination provisions of Section 504 of the Rehabilitation Act?

The Justice Department's career lawyers in the Civil Rights Division—that unit within Justice that usually handles an inquiry on civil rights questions such as this—prepared a draft opinion recommending that persons with AIDS, persons with ARC, and asymptomatic persons with HIV infection all be covered by the terms of Section 504. The recommendation extended as well to those merely perceived as infected with HIV.

For whatever reason and by whatever means, the draft opinion from the career staff of the Civil Rights Division was leaked to the media. Apparently, neither the substance of the draft opinion nor the tactic of leaking the draft opinion sat well with higher-ups at Justice.

The Reagan administration's Civil Rights Division was never known for its aggressiveness in pursuing civil rights; rather, most of the civil rights community, including this author, who served with the Civil Rights Division for the first year of the Reagan administration, felt that the division went far toward effectively dismantling the civil rights enforcement system that it had taken successive administrations under both parties to build and establish as a governmental institution. The division's approach to this issue was a classic example of the lengths to which it would go and the degrees to which it would complicate seemingly simple issues.

When the Justice Department's advice to the Department of Health and Human Services emerged as a final document, it came not from the Civil Rights Division's career staff. It came instead from the department's far more politically sensitive Office of Legal Counsel. Digesting too many pages of illogic, the opinion boiled down to people who suffer discrimination because of AIDS or related infections being able to seek relief under Section 504. But with barely a pause to breathe, it went on to say that Section 504 did not protect those who suffer discrimination based on fear of contagion, regardless of how irrational that fear may be.[2]

The department's opinion brushed aside overwhelming evidence from the Centers for Disease Control and others; it ignored the medical community's strong and virtually unanimous conclusions that casual, nonsexual contact poses no threat or risk of transmission, calling those conclusions "too sweeping"; it accepted the "natural tendency to err on the safe side"; and it left the complaining party with the burden of showing that his or her continued participation in a federally assisted program or activity would not jeopardize the health of others—reversing the traditional placement of burden of proof in civil rights cases.

Though technically directed to HHS in response to its inquiry, the Justice Department's opinion was seen as effectively binding on all executive branch departments and agencies unless and until overruled by the courts. The Justice Department's opinion was rendered in July 1986 and was met with nearly universal criticism, if not outright ridicule, by the community specifically interested in AIDS issues, by the larger civil rights community, and by the great bulk of the legal profession.

As the Justice Department considered this issue, several key cases were unfolding in the background. Broward County, Florida, became the first unit of government to fire a nonteacher public employee because of AIDS. In September 1984, 28-year-old budget analyst Todd Shuttleworth returned from a medical leave of absence to find on his desk a can of Lysol and a notice terminating his employment. Represented by the local chapter of the American Civil Liberties Union, he filed a formal complaint with the Florida Commission on Human Relations, alleging discrimination on the basis of handicap.[3] After the commission failed to rule within the time specified in the statutory scheme, Shuttleworth filed suit in federal court, alleging essentially the same claim.[4]

In Massachusetts, another case began to unfold as Paul Cronan repeatedly took medical time off from his job with New England Telephone and Telegraph. His supervisor required him to disclose the reason for the medical appointments before being allowed to miss additional time from work, and on learning that Cronan had AIDS, the supervisor advised Cronan's coworkers. Fearing for his safety, Cronan was unable to return to work, and he filed suit, alleging discrimination on the basis of handicap, among other grounds.[5]

In north Florida, Gene Arline had been terminated from a teaching position after a recurrence of a tuberculosis-related problem. She had filed suit, alleging discrimination on the basis of handicap under Section 504. The claim had gone up to the U.S. Court of Appeals, which had reversed lower findings and held that firing Arline would indeed constitute discrimination on the basis of handicap.[6] The ruling meant that a court of this significant level had for the first time found a contagious disease to be a handicap within the meaning of Section 504. The case went up on appeal to the U.S. Supreme Court, and all of the civil rights and AIDS-interested communities recognized that a ruling in Arline would have enormous spillover effect—if not direct precedent—on AIDS cases.

It was against this background that the Justice Department rendered its opinion to HHS. Within a month, HHS charged a North Carolina hospital with AIDS-based discrimination in violation of Section 504 for refusing to reemploy a registered nurse after he was diagnosed with AIDS.[7] The action of HHS clearly conflicted with the Justice Department's opinion. It demonstrated disagreement with, if not outright contempt for, Justice's convoluted and seemingly highly politicized "legal reasoning."

In December 1985—even before the Justice Department's opinion was rendered—the Florida Commission on Human Relations found that there was probable cause to believe that Shuttleworth had suffered unlawful employment discrimination on the basis of handicap, thus issuing the first ruling that AIDS discrimination came within the terms of Section 504.[8] A ruling in his federal court case when the judge denied the county's motion to dismiss signaled the same reasoning.[9] And in the Cronan case, a trial judge ruled that AIDS was a handicap within the meaning of a state law with language parallel to that of Section 504.[10] The case was eventually settled.

In March 1987, the U.S. Supreme Court ruled in the Arline case.[11] It ruled in favor of the handicapped teacher, calling her contagious disease just that—a handicap. The Court was well aware of the AIDS implications of its decision. Its ruling constituted a thorough rejection of the reasoning in the Justice Department's opinion. It said that infectiousness was relevant only to whether the employee was, as required by the language of the statute, "otherwise qualified" to perform the job. Directly addressing AIDS only in a footnote in the opinion, the Court said it was not deciding "the questions whether a carrier of a contagious disease such as AIDS could be considered to have a physical impairment, or whether such a person could be considered, solely on the basis of contagiousness, a handicapped person as defined" in the Rehabilitation Act. Nevertheless, the implication that PWAs would be protected as handicapped persons was clear to all, particularly in light of the lopsidedness of the seven-to-two vote in this case.

HIV employment issues continue to arise, as the Arline decision certainly did not address every unique possible question. Just months after that decision, a complaint was filed in Louisiana by a licensed practical nurse discharged for refusing to take an HIV-antibody test following the AIDS-related death of the nurse's roommate.[12] At the same time, a New Mexico nurse was discharged for being HIV-positive.[13]

Then, in November 1987, came an important ruling in the Chalk case[14] (discussed in detail in Chapter 7). Chalk's attorneys had sought a preliminary injunction against his being removed from the classroom, and the judge in the trial court denied the request. The negative impact of that ruling was short-lived, however, in light of the court's noted ruling in favor of reinstating Chalk. Again, this case marked the first time that the federal appeals courts had ruled that AIDS itself came squarely within the protection of Section 504.

And in March 1988, the U.S. Office of Personnel Management issued guidelines for federal workplace treatment of

PWAs.[15] The guidelines recognized that casual contact poses no threat of transmission of HIV and said that PWAs should be allowed to work as long as they are able. A few months later, even the Department of Justice finally reversed its earlier and most controversial opinion on the subject.[16]

In treating this issue of employment discrimination, one must understand that employers are not locked into the employment relationship forever. To be considered as not discriminating on the basis of handicap, employers must make what the law calls "reasonable accommodations."[17] Those are the kinds of changes you have already seen in the workplace and in society in general—the curb cuts, the braille elevator numbers, the adaptation of toilet facilities to accommodate those who may be wheelchair-bound, and so on. Reasonable accommodations can also include flexible work hours, an opportunity for a periodic rest while at work, or time off for medical appointments, as examples of some of those most frequently used for persons with HIV disease.

In general, though, the nondiscrimination provision in Section 504 and similarly worded provisions in other federal, state, and local laws and ordinances are not regarded as absolutely protecting persons with AIDS, persons with ARC, and those with asymptomatic HIV infection. New issues as well as the old ones have continued to arise as employers resist compliance with these laws out of financial considerations, prejudice, or both and as employees keep pursuing their now well-established rights under the nondiscrimination laws. Let's look at some of the more significant of those cases that were decided after the decisions in the Shuttleworth, Cronan, Arline, Chalk, and other early cases.

As to whether these laws even apply, there is a split of opinion regarding those only perceived as being infected with HIV. The New York Supreme Court (which is not that state's highest court despite the court's name) ruled in a 1991 case brought by a man who was fired because his employer thought he had AIDS that that state's Human Rights Law covers perceived as well as actual disabilities.[18] But the Michigan Court of Appeals went in the other direction, saying that the Michigan Handicapped Civil Rights Act does not apply to those only perceived as and not actually handicapped and that the remedy for this gap was in the hands of the legislature.[19]

In a strange twist to the cases on this issue, a woman in Texas filed suit against her employer after she was dismissed because she volunteered during off-duty hours at the Houston AIDS Foundation. The Texas court found that she was not covered within the Texas law protecting the handicapped from employment discrimination, and she has appealed to the state's supreme court.[20]

Once HIV infection is real rather than just perceived, there seems to be no dissent from affording protection under the various laws that provide for nondiscrimination on the basis of handicap. Still, though, new questions arise. In 1990, the U.S. Office of Civil Rights within the Department of Health and Human Services issued a finding that an employer's denial of employment to a pharmacist based on the pharmacist's HIV infection violated Section 504.[21] The New York Division of Human Rights issued an initial ruling that recommended the pharmacist be allowed to have the position without being allowed to carry out invasive procedures, but a later alternative proposed order eliminated that restriction.[22] The next chapter of the seemingly never-ending saga of this case occurred when the hospital requested reopening of the case in light of the CDC report of possible transmission of HIV from dentist to patient in Florida.[23] Next, the New York Human Rights Division ordered the hospital to pay the pharmacist $30,000 in damages, offer him with back pay the next available position similar to the one that was denied, and initiate comprehensive education about employment discrimination law for all administrative employees.[24] And finally, HHS announced that its Office of Civil Rights was ready to enter the enforcement phase of the case.[25]

HIV infection was real to 27 people who applied for jobs at Montfort Inc.'s pork processing plant in Minnesota. Job applicants were required to test for HIV antibodies, according to officials of the company, because plant employees use knives and could expose each other to HIV through cuts. The state human rights commissioner said that use of the tests violated the state's antibias laws, and the parties agreed to settle for payments by the company of $100,000 to each of the 27 applicants denied a job because of being HIV-positive, with the company being further obligated to hire them to fill vacancies as they occur.[26]

And an employer in a Virginia suburb of Washington, DC, tried in a novel way to get out from under an HIV-related employment discrimination claim. The employer's defense was that the HIV-infected window dresser was an independent contractor rather than a full-time employee and was therefore not protected by the law. The City of Alexandria Human Rights Commission disagreed.[27]

Most of the more current HIV-related employment issues seem to occur once the employee has already been hired. Occupational hazards were the cause of a suit against the New York City Transit Authority, where the state's attorney general sought special training regarding HIV safety for transit employees in light of used drug paraphernalia and human waste regularly found throughout the transit system. The suit resulted in settlement agreed upon by both parties.[28]

Apparently, there is some effectiveness to attention to occupational hazards and training and safety measures. According to a mid-1990 news report, the Chicken Ranch Brothel in Pahrump, Nevada, is "an island of safe sex in a sea of disease." Researchers examined the results of sexually transmissible disease tests, including 849 HIV-antibody tests, with no positive results since 1986, the year when condom use became the law in the 35 legal brothels in Nevada.[29]

Once the employee is hired and adequately trained, we come to the employee's role in working for the employer. In one case on this issue, an HIV-infected physician sued the FBI for violating his constitutional rights by refusing to send prospective agents to him for physical examinations and for investigating the doctor's HIV status after he assured the bureau that he posed no threat to patients. The suit was dismissed for lack of "standing" to sue the U.S. government under Section 504,[30] but the dismissal has been appealed[31] and reportedly overturned, thus allowing the case to proceed.[32]

In another case on the issue of the employee's role, an interstate legal service firm was found to have violated the Pennsylvania Human Relations Act by removing an attorney from his position as regional partner just a week after the employee was diagnosed with AIDS.[33]

And of course, we encounter in this context the seemingly always controversial issue of persons with HIV infection in food-handling positions.[34] The corporate owners of the Cut Mart convenience-store chain were ordered by the Missouri Commission on Human Rights to pay a former employee $5,000 for emotional distress and humiliation resulting from the employee's removal from a food-handling position in 1987 because the manager feared that the employee had AIDS.[35]

In April 1991, a New Jersey court approved of limiting an employee's role because of AIDS. The case was brought by the estate of a physician whose surgical privileges were suspended after he was diagnosed with AIDS. The judge said that doctors with AIDS should stop performing procedures that would pose a risk to patients.[36] Unless the ruling is successfully appealed, it will stand as the first on record in support of limiting the rights of any kind of employee because of HIV disease.[37] A full chapter on the right of patients and medical/dental service providers to know whether the other is infected with HIV concludes this book.

Then we get to the question of whether the employer made the legally required "reasonable accommodations." One noteworthy case on that issue found for the employer. It involved a fire fighter who was placed on light duty and then suspended until ultimate termination. A federal court dismissed the fire fighter's allegations of unlawful employment discrimination, saying that these steps were an effort to help the fire fighter, particularly where the fire fighter had repeatedly refused offers to return to regular duty.[38]

And finally, we get to terminations. Sadly, there are still plenty to report. One case saw a New York court affirm a ruling by the commissioner of the New York Division of Human Rights that a restaurant unlawfully discriminated by firing a waiter shortly after he disclosed to a superior that he suffered from AIDS-Related Complex (ARC).[39]

An Illinois restaurant agreed to a $10,000 settlement, believed to have been the first under the state's Human Rights Act, in a case involving an HIV bias claim by a waiter who said he was fired after telling a superior of his HIV-positive status.[40]

Ruling that the deception was not serious enough to justify dismissal and appeared designed to protect the employee's privacy and not to harm the employer, a state appeals court awarded unemployment compensation to a salesman fired because he did not tell his employer that he had AIDS.[41]

A flight attendant filed an administrative complaint against his airline employer alleging that he was fired because he is an HIV-positive homosexual. The complaint was filed in a jurisdiction that affords protection on the bases of sexual orientation as well as HIV status. The airline told the employee that his job termination was due to a report of his having stolen cocktail money; however, the employee has asserted that he was working on the flight in question in the first class cabin where no money is collected from passengers and that the employment of others alleged to have been involved in the theft was not terminated.[42]

An applicant who had already passed extensive physical and background examinations and was offered a job as a fire fighter sued the District of Columbia Fire Department when it revoked its offer after he voluntarily disclosed his HIV-positive status to a superior.[43]

A fire fighter position was also the subject of what may be the first worker's compensation settlement for a person with AIDS. Although there was no acknowledgment that the illness was an "on-the-job disease," a Hallandale, Florida, fire fighter/emergency medical technician received $45,000 in worker's compensation benefits under the settlement.[44]

And these cases are surely not limited to traditional, mainstream businesses. The Minnesota Department of Human Rights ordered the owner of an adult book store to pay $70,000 in fines and fees for firing an HIV-positive employee because he believed the employee, of whom he had by publicly posted notices required the HIV-antibody test, had AIDS.[45] "To countenance discrimination such as that set out in this case is to permit fear and prejudice to prevail over reason," wrote the administrative law judge. "The relief ordered . . . is directed at ensuring that [the complainant] is viewed according to his capabilities rather than his disability. The outrageousness of [the employer's] conduct, as well as the resulting serious harm, fully justifies the substantial damages awarded in this matter."[46]

A hopeful sign was made public in April 1991 with the announcement by the Citizens Commission on AIDS for New York City and northern New Jersey that a document pledging assistance to HIV-infected employees and guaranteeing their rights in the workplace has been endorsed by some 600 employers nationwide. Surveyed employers recognized that their involvement in HIV/AIDS in terms of time and money would at least remain at current levels and might increase.[47]

NOTES

1. 29 U.S.C. 794.

2. See *AIDS Update*, Lambda Legal Defense and Education Fund, Inc., No. 8 (July 1986), pp. 4–6.

3. *Shuttleworth v. Broward County Office of Budget and Management Policy*, No. 85–0624, Fla. Commission on Human Relations (December 11, 1985).

4. *Shuttleworth v. Broward County*, S.D. Fla., No. 85–6623–Civ., filed August 12, 1985.

5. *Cronan v. New England Tel. Co.*, 41 FEP Cases 1273 (MA Super. Ct. 1986).

6. *Arline v. School Bd. of Nassau County*, 772 F.2d 759 (11th Cir. 1985).

7. See *AIDS Update*, Lambda Legal Defense and Education Fund, Inc., No. 9 (August 1986), pp. 4–5.

8. See n. 3, *supra*.

9. See n. 4, *supra*.

10. See n. 5, *supra*.

11. *School Bd. of Nassau County, Fla. v. Arline*, 480 U.S. 273 (1987).

12. *Leckelt v. Board of Commissioners of Hospital District No.*

1, 714 F.Supp. 1377 (E.D. La. 1989), aff'd No. 89–3256, 5th Cir., August 28, 1990. See *AIDS Lit. Rptr.*, February 9, 1990, p. 3998, and September 14, 1990, p. 5020.

13. See *AIDS Update*, Lambda Legal Defense and Education Fund, Inc., No. 14 (January 1987), pp. 1–2.

14. *Chalk v. United States District Court of Cal.*, 840 F.2d 701 (9th Cir. 1988).

15. Office of Personnel Management Guidelines, BNA, Daily Labor Report, March 23, 1988, No. 50, p. D–1.

16. Justice Department Memorandum on the Application of the Rehabilitation Act's Section 504 to HIV-Infected Persons, Daily Labor Report, No. 195, pp. D1–D11, September 27, 1988.

17. See n. 1, *supra*.

18. *Romei v. Shell Oil Co.*, NY Sup. Ct., N.Y. Cty., N.Y.L.J., February 22, 1991, as reported in *AIDS Policy and Law*, Vol. 6, No. 4 (March 6, 1991), p. 4.

19. *Sanchez v. Kostas Lagoudakis, d/b/a/ Paradise Family Restaurant et al.*, MI Ct. of App., No. 115526. See *AIDS Lit. Rptr.*, July 13, 1990, p. 4748.

20. *Brunner v. Al Attar et al.*, TX Sup. Ct., No. C–9772. See *AIDS Lit. Rptr.*, June 8, 1990, p. 4612, and *AIDS Update*, Lambda Legal Defense and Education Fund, Inc., Vol. 4, No. 2 (July 1990), p. 4.

21. *Doe v. Westchester County Medical Center.* See *AIDS Lit. Rptr.*, April 13, 1990, p. 4287.

22. *Ibid.*, NY Div. of Human Rights, N.Y. City, Nos. 1B–E–D–86–116054, 1B–P–S–87–117683. See *AIDS Lit. Rptr.*, August 24, 1990, p. 4955.

23. See *AIDS Lit. Rptr.*, October 26, 1990, p. 5250.

24. See *AIDS Lit. Rptr.*, December 28, 1990, p. 5534.

25. See *AIDS Lit. Rptr.*, January 25, 1991, p. 5706.

26. *The Advocate*, No. 577 (May 21, 1991), p. 27.

27. *Nickles v. Steven-Windsor, Inc.*, City of Alexandria Human Rights Commission, Alexandria, Va., No. E10–4323. See *AIDS Lit. Rptr.*, September 14, 1990, p. 5025.

28. *New York v. NYC Transit Authority*, NY Sup. Ct., N.Y. Cty., No. 41627/90. See *AIDS Lit. Rptr.*, August 10, 1990, p. 4906, and *AIDS Update*, Lambda Legal Defense and Education Fund, Inc., Vol. 4, No. 2 (July 1990), p. 2.

29. See "AIDS Notes," *The Weekly News*, July 4, 1990, p. 30.

30. *Doe v. Attorney General of the United States*, N.D. Ca., No. C–88–3820. See *AIDS Lit. Rptr.*, October 13, 1989, p. 3418.

31. *Ibid.*, 9th Cir., Nos. 89–15933, 89–16134. See *AIDS Lit. Rptr.*, June 22, 1990, p. 4689.

32. *The Advocate*, No. 585 (September 10, 1991), p. 26.

33. *Cain v. Hyatt Legal Services*, E.D. Pa., CIV.A 88–6665. See *AIDS Update*, Lambda Legal Defense and Education Fund, Inc., Vol. 4, No. 2, (July 1990), p. 3.

34. See Chapter 21, "The Americans with Disabilities Act."

35. *McClanahan v. Rose City Oil*, MO Comm. on Human Rights, ME–3/87–5830. See *AIDS Lit. Rptr.*, September 28, 1990, p. 5103.

36. "Judge Cites AIDS Risk," *Fort Lauderdale Sun-Sentinel*, April 26, 1991, p. 3A.

37. *Estate of William Behringer v. The Medical Center at Princeton et al.*, NJ Super. Ct., Law Div., Mercer Cty., No. L88–2550. See *AIDS Lit. Rptr.*, May 10, 1991, p. 6245.

38. *Severino v. North Fort Myers Fire Control District et al.*, M.D. Fla., No. 88–142–CIV–FTM–13B. See *AIDS Lit. Rptr.*, October 12, 1990, p. 5168.

39. *Club Swamp Annex v. White*, NY Sup. Ct., App. Div., 2nd Jud. Dept. See *AIDS Lit. Rptr.*, December 14, 1990, p. 5484.

40. See *AIDS Lit. Rptr.*, June 24, 1991, p. 6473.

41. *Hummer v. Unemployment Appeals Commission*, No. 90–271, 1991 WL 1090 (Fla. App. 1991). See *AIDS Update*, Lambda Legal Defense and Education Fund, Inc., Vol. 4, No. 4 (March 1991), p. 11, and *The Advocate*, No. 571 (February 26, 1991), p. 26.

42. *Olinger v. Midway Airlines*, IL Dept. of Human Relations, June 27, 1991; *Olinger v. Midway Airlines*, Chicago Commission on Human Relations, No. 91–E–0079. See *AIDS Lit. Rptr.*, July 26, 1991, p. 6599. See also "Midway Bias Claim May Be First Test of Chicago Panel," *The Advocate*, No. 581 (July 16, 1991), p. 22.

43. *Doe v. District of Columbia, District of Columbia Fire Department*, D DC, No. 91–1641. See *AIDS Lit. Rptr.*, July 26, 1991, p. 6598.

44. "Fire fighter with AIDS to get Worker's Comp Settlement," *Fort Lauderdale Sun-Sentinel*, July 25, 1991, p. 5B.

45. *State of Minnesota v. DiMa Corp.*, Richard Carriveau, MN Off. of Admin. Hearings, MN Dept. of Human Rights, No. 1–1700–4899–2, DHR–E18951. See *AIDS Lit. Rptr.*, January 11, 1991, p. 5622.

46. "Gay Man Wins Damages for HIV Discrimination," *The Weekly News*, December 19, 1990, p. 8.

47. See *AIDS Lit. Rptr.*, April 12, 1991, pp. 6095–6.

9

Family Law

Family law is the name now more commonly used for what was previously called domestic relations law. It includes prenuptial agreements, the validity of marriages, annulments, divorces (now frequently called dissolutions of marriage), and custody and visitation rights. One might logically ask how HIV disease would relate to this area of law. Unfortunately, some of the saddest examples of the circle-the-wagons mentality afford the answer.

One of the earliest cases involved an HIV-infected Puerto Rican man who was actually prohibited by a court order from kissing his own children.[1] In 1986, two other issues arose in Illinois. In one case, a court ordered a father to submit to HIV-antibody testing before allowing him overnight visitation rights with his child. That court order was ultimately overturned.[2] In the other case, a court ruled that the ex-husband of a nurse who cared for AIDS patients acted reasonably in denying the nurse visitation rights with her children and in asking her to take an HIV-antibody test.[3]

At about the same time in Indiana, a court barred a man

from seeing his two-year-old child because the man had tested positive for HIV and was therefore "a danger to the minor child's well-being." The ruling was criticized by an official of the Indiana Department of Health, and the judge then threatened that official with a contempt citation.[4]

Some states have taken a more enlightened approach to these issues through the legislative process. In Florida, for example, state law prohibits courts from denying shared parental responsibility, custody, or visitation rights to a parent or grandparent because that parent or grandparent is or is believed to be HIV-positive.[5]

And some courts have begun to get educated in even this specialty area. In 1987, an Ohio trial court denied a request for an order to require a gay father to submit to HIV-antibody testing as a condition for visitation.[6] And in early 1988, a New York court denied a motion to compel a father to test for HIV antibodies when it ruled on a custody issue.[7] In August 1988, a Maryland court awarded physical custody jointly to a child's mother and gay father with AIDS.[8]

In a case in which a mother and former wife had repeatedly denied visitation to her former husband, the children's HIV-infected father, a Tennessee court enforced previous court orders allowing such visitation rights.[9] When those orders were still ignored and the mother absconded with the children, the court issued a suspended jail sentence and a fine for contempt.[10] And noting that "[n]umerous studies have found no risk of HIV infections through close personal contact or sharing of household functions," a New York court held that the mere fact that a divorced mother is HIV-positive is not sufficient grounds for granting custody of her infant child to the father.[11]

An intermediate appellate court in Indiana reversed a trial judge's approval of a divorce settlement that awarded the former wife 60% of the couple's property based on her fear of contracting AIDS from her former husband because of his homosexual relationships. The court said that a settlement based on a determination of fault violated the state's divorce laws.[12]

In an effort to further judicial education about AIDS, the

American Bar Association has begun a special project, working through the National Judicial College in Reno, Nevada. However, that one small institution can only begin the process of education of the thousands of judges at the local, state, and federal levels throughout the United States and sitting at both the trial and appellate levels about the legal issues related to AIDS.

The ABA's Policy on AIDS makes clear that that organization feels HIV status should not generally be deemed admissible evidence in a family law proceeding. Moreover, the ABA has said that HIV status should be considered only in the same manner as other medical conditions and that HIV status should not be deemed admissible evidence for the purpose of proving a party's sexual orientation.[13]

And it appears that at least some within the judicial system are accepting the ABA's guidance and judicial education on this subject. In a significant treatment of these issues, Justice Kristen Booth Glen of the New York State Supreme Court for New York City pointed out to her colleagues on the bench that in states where cruelty, cruel and inhuman treatment, or any similar characterizations constitute grounds for divorce, "the fact that an HIV-positive spouse has engaged in unprotected sexual relations without notifying his or her partner of the infection may well constitute grounds for divorce."[14] She went on to conclude that the applicable test in custody cases "should be drawn from the analogous area of parents with physical disabilities" with the law suggesting that "a handicap is not, in and of itself, grounds for denying or modifying custody, but rather it must be considered only insofar as it actually affects the child or children in question [citations omitted] . . . As with most issues in custody and visitation, the overriding concern must be 'the best interests of the child,'" she concluded.[15]

NOTES

1. *G.R.M. v. J.R.A.*, Superior Court of Puerto Rico. See also *AIDS Update*, Lambda Legal Defense and Education Fund, Inc., No. 8 (July 1986), p. 6.

2. See *AIDS Update*, Lambda Legal Defense and Education Fund, Inc., No. 8 (July 1986), p. 6. Order vacated for procedural reasons and motion later withdrawn. *AIDS Update*, Lambda Legal Defense and Education Fund, Inc., No. 11 (October 1986), pp. 11–12.

3. *Buck v. Grien*, IL Cir. Ct. See *AIDS Update*, Lambda Legal Defense and Education Fund, Inc., No. 10 (September 1986), pp. 7–8.

4. See *AIDS Update*, Lambda Legal Defense and Education Fund, Inc., No. 12 (November 1986), p. 8.

5. Section 61.13, Florida Statutes (1989).

6. *In the Matter of Smalley*, No. 83–112, Dom. Rel. Ct., Muskingum Co., filed December 1986. See *AIDS Update*, Lambda Legal Defense and Education Fund, Inc., Vol. 2., No. 1 (June/July 1987), p. 4.

7. *Doe v. Roe*, NY Sup. Ct., N.Y. Cty., Index No. 103035/88, N.Y.L.J., March 16, 1988.

8. *Doe v. Roe*, MD Cir. Ct., Montgomery Cty., No. 28094, May 4, 1988.

9. *Tubb v. Tubb*, TN Chancery Ct., Wilson Cty., No. 3306. See *AIDS Lit. Rptr.*, January 22, 1990, p. 4688.

10. *Id.* See *AIDS Lit. Rptr.*, October 26, 1990, p. 5254.

11. *Matter of Steven L.*, NY Fam. Ct., Kings Cty., October 3, 1990. See *ABA Journal*, January 1991, p. 80.

12. *R.E.G. v. L.M.G.*, IN Ct. of App., 1st Dist., No. 32A01–91–CV–9. See *AIDS Lit. Rptr.*, June 14, 1991, p. 6389.

13. "Policy on AIDS," adopted by the American Bar Association, August 1989.

14. Glen, Justice Kristen Booth, "Parents with AIDS, Children with AIDS," *The Judges' Journal*, Vol. 29, No. 2 (Spring 1990), p. 17.

15. *Ibid.* at pp. 17–18.

10

Free Speech

The First Amendment to the U.S. Constitution guarantees one of our nation's most precious rights. Yet even this cherished liberty has come under attack with the advent of AIDS and the fear and ignorance with which policymakers have dealt with it.

Education has been almost universally viewed as the most effective weapon against the spread of HIV disease. And in order to be most effective, such education must be aimed at all people, particularly those most likely to engage in high-risk behavior. Yet in mid-1990, the Illinois Senate approved legislation to prevent the Chicago Transit Authority from displaying, in donated space, safe-sex posters that show same-sex couples kissing. Proponents of the legislation said that the posters condoned homosexuality.[1]

The First Amendment came into indirect play when a Lee County, Florida, judge discriminated on the basis of AIDS in her courtroom, expressing horror and anger that a PWA would risk spread of HIV by coming into her courtroom and summarily evicting him from there. Present for a hearing on a traffic charge, the PWA was sentenced while he was out of the courtroom, violating another basic principle of the American legal process. An AIDS activist attorney filed a formal grievance against the judge and was immediately warned that complaints against Florida judges could not be discussed publicly. Wishing to ensure that PWAs and all persons in Florida understood their rights to complain against unfair or discriminatory actions by judges, the lawyer sued and had the "gag rule" declared an unconstitutional abridgement of free speech.[2] As was noted in Chapter 2, "Access to Justice," whether because of the grievance filed against her or for other reasons, that judge resigned from the bench within several months of the filing of the complaint.

In Pennsylvania, members of the activist group ACT-UP sued the state police seeking an order to halt alleged attempts to infiltrate their organization and keep them from demonstrating at public events, including the inauguration of a new governor.[3] Noting that closure of the House gallery out of fear of disruption of the governor's address would be "the spitting image of an improper prior restraint—an attempt to restrain free speech prior to publication or dissemination," the court denied the group's motion for a preliminary injunction as the proper party to sue, the Speaker of the Pennsylvania House, was not before the court.[4]

An Illinois woman sued two newspapers in July 1991 for reporting that she was ordered by a court to take an HIV-antibody test after she was arrested for prostitution. At issue is a state law that prohibits public disclosure of HIV-antibody test results. The newspapers contend that the law violates constitutional guarantees of free speech.[5]

And the U.S. Supreme Court rejected without comment the appeal of a California woman who claimed that she had been unconstitutionally dismissed from her position on the Los Angeles County Commission on Obscenity and Pornography because of her opposition to specific AIDS education materials. In an interesting use of the First Amendment from multiple directions, she had claimed that the materials were obscene and sought to have them banned. When she was dismissed, she alleged that this was a violation of her First

Amendment free speech rights. The state courts, however, ruled that she was a political appointee and was therefore subject to the power of her governmental supervisor, and it was that ruling that the U.S. Supreme Court declined to disturb.[6]

NOTES

1. *The Advocate*, No. 556 (July 31, 1990), p. 18.

2. *Terl v. Florida Judicial Qualifications Commission*, S.D. Fla., No. 89-6362-CIV-Marcus. See *AIDS Lit. Rptr.*, October 24, 1990, p. 5244.

3. *ACT-UP v. Walp et al.*, M.D. Pa., No. 1:CV-91-0148. See *AIDS Lit. Rptr.*, February 8, 1991, p. 5790.

4. *Id.* See *AIDS Lit. Rptr.*, March 8, 1991, p. 5926.

5. *The Advocate*, No. 584 (August 27, 1991), p. 27.

6. *Kennedy v. County of Los Angeles*, U.S. Sup. Ct., Oct. Term, 1990, No. 90-784. See *AIDS Lit. Rptr.*, February 22, 1991, p. 5849.

11

Housing

Housing is deemed by many to be a basic right. When HIV infection—or even traits associated with members of groups stereotyped as being at high risk for HIV infection—becomes entangled with housing issues, housing has been shamefully treated as something much less than a basic right.

Examples of discrimination in this area abound. In a case that lasted some three years, a group of doctors had contracted to purchase a co-op in New York. The contract required the sponsor of the sale to pursue change-of-use permission to convert the premises to medical offices. When the sponsor learned that the doctors would be treating PWAs, it refused to proceed with the change-of-use filing, thereby frustrating the doctors' purchase. The sponsor claimed that the doctors had committed fraud by not disclosing the nature of the practice, and it sought to sell the unit to a third party instead. An appellate court granted an order temporarily restraining the sale to the third party and later issued an injunction to the same effect. Ultimately, a jury awarded the doctors punitive damages, and that award was upheld by the court.[1]

As early in the AIDS chronology as 1986, the Boston Fair Housing Commission banned discrimination in housing against persons with AIDS or related medical conditions, and that ban extended to both the sale and rental of housing. Even inquiry regarding HIV status was made unlawful.[2]

In New Jersey in 1987, it took a court's preliminary injunction to restrain a landlord from renting to others an apartment that he had refused to rent to three gay males because of the landlord's fear of AIDS.[3]

And in New York in early 1988, the Human Rights Commission awarded $15,000 in damages to a dentist whose landlord, also a dentist, terminated his sublease because the tenant-dentist treated PWAs. The action was deemed discrimination on the basis of handicap. The award was ultimately reduced to $5,000, but it was upheld by the appellate court.[4]

Another court in New York granted a motion to dismiss a legal action in which a couple was trying to rescind its purchase of a co-op because the couple had not been told that the prior owner had AIDS.[5]

Not all attempts to stop denial of housing on the basis of HIV infection or high-risk stereotyping have met such success, however. The most notable jurisdiction trying to go in the opposite direction has been Texas. There, litigation to void a contract because the buyers were not told about the seller's AIDS-related illness generated national attention. In April 1988, the Texas Association of Realtors issued guidelines advising real estate brokers and agents to inform potential home buyers if a residence was previously occupied by a person with AIDS.[6]

The reaction to the Texas situation was to generate legislation to prohibit just such factors from being considered in real estate transactions. One section of the Florida Omnibus AIDS Act, for example, provides that the fact that the occupant of real property was HIV-positive need not be disclosed in real estate transactions and that the failure to make such a disclosure does not give rise to a cause of action for damages.[7] The provision was a direct outgrowth of the Texas squabble.

Reaction to the Texas litigation and industry guidelines also helped push through the Federal Fair Housing Amendments Act of 1988,[8] which bans discrimination against persons with disabilities, including AIDS and HIV-related medical conditions. The act applies to virtually all housing in the United States and took effect in March of 1989. Just six months later, a U.S. District Court in Illinois issued a preliminary injunction requiring the city of Belleville to allow the opening of a home for PWAs over the city's strong objections, thus, for the first time enforcing the act's application to persons with AIDS and other disabilities.[9]

And the corporate owner of a Georgia apartment complex has been sued under the Fair Housing Act as a result of allegations that the resident manager ordered a tenant's guest from the swimming pool because the guest had AIDS.[10]

In a case reminiscent of the Texas situation, an Alabama purchaser of a house sued because he had not been told that the prior owner died of complications from AIDS. He contended that the cause of death of the seller reduced the value of the home. A jury rejected his claim for $600,000 in damages.[11]

Housing issues also sometimes take more subtle, less directly recognizable forms. For example, in June 1990, a federal court enjoined a local Puerto Rico zoning board from rejecting placement of an AIDS hospice because the area was zoned for agricultural purposes. While the planned AIDS hospice had no agricultural purpose, the area was already populated by several businesses, a factory, and residences.[12]

Not so subtle was action by the U.S. Department of Housing and Urban Development (HUD), which had twice rejected an application for low-interest financing of housing for the handicapped, specifically a 24-unit housing plan targeted to serve Santa Clara, California, residents with AIDS. Among HUD's positions were that HIV-infected persons did not qualify as "handicapped" and that the illness was not "expected to be one of long-continued and indefinite duration." With help from a public policy advocacy group, the applicant filed suit, with the suit having seen settled in 1991. The applicant agreed not to restrict residency in the project only to persons with AIDS or ARC and to judge entrance eligibility on a case-by-case basis in accordance with HUD regulations.[13]

In yet another example of indirect discrimination, the pastor of a Catholic church in the District of Columbia yielded to complaints from congregants by withdrawing permission for an AIDS support and prayer group to meet in the church basement after church members placed angry notes in the collection plate and wrote irate letters.[14]

Similarly, in June 1991, a Roman Catholic order abandoned its plan to open an AIDS hospice in a rural part of Georgia. The decision was the result of community pressure, led by the local county commission.[15]

Not so indirect was the response to the federal court order that directed the public school system in De Soto County, Florida, to admit the sons of the Ray family, all three of whom were infected with HIV as a result of medication for their hemophilia. Their home in Arcadia was the subject of a "fire-bombing." Charges that could be brought in that case might include deprivation of federal civil rights in addition to arson.[16]

And in another example of enforcement by the federal government of the new law on this subject, the U.S. Justice Department charged in early 1991 that an Indianapolis apartment complex and its operating partner had violated the Fair Housing Amendments Act by denying a residency application to an HIV-infected man and that it "refused to make reasonable accommodations" that might have afforded him the opportunity to live at the complex. The defendants have denied the charges.[17]

NOTES

1. *Seitzman v. Hudson River Associates,* NY Sup. Ct., N.Y. Cty., N.Y.L.J. May 5, 1989.

2. See *AIDS Update,* Lambda Legal Defense and Education Fund, Inc., No. 12 (November 1986), p. 11.

3. See *AIDS Update,* Lambda Legal Defense and Education Fund, Inc., No. 17 (April 1987), p. 1.

4. *Barton v. New York City Commission on Human Rights,* NY App. Div., 1st Dept., No. 36897, N.Y.L.J. June 8, 1989.

5. *Kleinfeld v. McAnally,* NY Sup. Ct., N.Y. Cty., Index No. 11181/88, N.Y.L.J. January 24, 1989.

6. See *AIDS Update,* Lambda Legal Defense and Education Fund, Inc., Vol. 2, No. 7 (April 1988), p. 4.

7. Sect. 689.25, Florida Statutes (1989).

8. 42 U.S.C. Sects. 3601 *et seq.*

9. *Baxter v. City of Belleville,* 720 F.Supp. 720 (S.D. Ill. 1989).

10. *Beasley v. Ken Edwards Enterprises, Inc., d/b/a/ Kenco-Briarcliff Apartments,* N.D. Ga., Atlanta Div., No. 1:91–CV–1348. See *AIDS Lit. Rptr.,* July 12, 1991, p. 6526.

11. *The Advocate,* No. 585 (September 10, 1991), p. 26.

12. *Association of Relatives and Friends of AIDS Patients et al. v. Regulations and Permits Administration et al.,* 740 F.Supp. 95 (D.P.R. 1990). See *AIDS Lit. Rptr.,* July 27, 1990, p. 4821, and *AIDS Update,* Lambda Legal Defense and Education Fund, Inc., Vol. 4, No. 2 (December 1990), p. 7.

13. *Jonathan Moreau, Robert Roe, Housing for Independent People v. Jack Kemp,* ND CA, No. C89–3469–FMS. See *AIDS Lit. Rptr.,* April 26, 1991, p. 6168.

14. *The Advocate,* Issue No. 569 (January 29, 1991), p. 20.

15. *The Advocate,* No. 582 (July 30, 1991), p. 28.

16. See Chapter 7, "Education."

17. *United States v. Georgetown Village Apartments et al.,* S.D. Ind., Indianapolis Div., No. IP 91 297C. See *AIDS Lit. Rptr.,* May 24, 1991, p. 6335.

12

Immigration

Immigration is a very specialized area of law with which few outside the legal profession—and even few inside it— have contact. Nevertheless, a quick look at legal issues affecting immigration and HIV will further the reader's understanding of how our society treats the HIV population.

Immigration is also another of those areas in which the federal government has exclusive jurisdiction and, as in the case of certain federal civilian employees and the U.S. military, has extended its interest in testing.

The regulation of immigration on the basis of contagious diseases dates to the adoption and ultimate codification in 1952, as part of the Immigration and Nationality Act (INA), of specific exclusions for aliens suffering from such contagious diseases as leprosy and tuberculosis. The provision was revised in 1961 to reflect changes in medical knowledge and to incorporate more precise language.[1] The language of the provision is that "aliens who are afflicted with any dangerous contagious disease" shall be excluded from the United States.[2]

Determination and designation of which diseases come within that statutory language are left to the U.S. Public Health Service. In mid-1987, the Public Health Service added "acquired immune deficiency syndrome (AIDS)" to the list of "dangerous contagious diseases."[3] Following through on that change, the Immigration and Naturalization Service (INS) referred for confirmatory blood tests immigrants exhibiting clinical symptoms of AIDS.[4]

Even before the Public Health Service finalized its rule on AIDS, however, Congress enacted the Supplemental Appropriations Act of 1987,[5] one section of which directed the president to use executive authority to add HIV infection to the list of "dangerous contagious diseases."[6] Known as the "Helms Amendment," the provision was sponsored by Senator Jesse Helms, a chronic foe of activists asserting the rights of persons with AIDS.

A system of waivers was made available for applicants for temporary admission as nonimmigrants for the purpose of receiving medical treatment, those seeking admission as refugees for humanitarian purposes, and those already residing in the United States and seeking legalization of their resident status. The system of waivers did not, however, apply to applicants for permanent residence, with only limited exceptions.[7]

Probably the single noteworthy case in this area of law is that of a Dutch representative to a lesbian and gay health conference. The conference was taking place in San Francisco, and the traveler sought to enter this country at Minneapolis-St. Paul. He was stopped there when the HIV treatment drug AZT was found in his briefcase. With the authorities acting under that provision of the Immigration and Naturalization Act which allows the INS to deny entry to a person with a "dangerous contagious disease," he was jailed in a county jail and not allowed to continue his entry in the United States in his effort to learn more about how best to care for his health. Local INS officials were reportedly willing to grant him a waiver and allow his entry into the United States, but the associate commissioner of the INS refused. The case became a rallying point for AIDS and gay rights activists, and an INS immigration judge ultimately reversed the denial and granted the man's request for a waiver of the exclusion.[8] INS filed an emergency request to stay execution of the order granting the waiver, but the Board of Immigration Appeals refused even to consider the request.[9]

The Bush administration seemed more amenable to recognizing the limited risk of transmission of HIV than was the Reagan administration, as was evidenced in a series of steps taken in 1990 and early 1991. In February of that year, the Centers for Disease Control recommended that AIDS and all other contagious diseases except tuberculosis (which can be spread through casual contact) be removed from the list of diseases used to bar people from entering the United States.[10]

As the time to convene the annual International Conference on AIDS neared in 1990, that conference having been located in San Francisco, the Bush administration announced a new ten-day visa for those traveling to professional, business, or scientific conferences deemed to be in the public interest. The move was reportedly aimed at defusing protests against the U.S. immigration policy by a threatened boycott of the conference. Applicants for the new visa did not have to reveal whether they were infected with HIV, as would otherwise have been their obligation.[11]

About a month later, in an opinion requested by a member of Congress regarded as a friend to those pursuing the rights of persons with AIDS, the acting U.S. comptroller general advised that the president did have the authority to remove HIV from the list of "dangerous contagious diseases" for which aliens can be prohibited from visiting the United States.[12]

In November 1990, President Bush signed into law a major overhaul in U.S. immigration laws, including the elimination of the automatic exclusion of what most newspapers called "AIDS sufferers" from legal status, leaving it to the U.S. Department of Health and Human Services to decide whether to list any degree of HIV disease as an excludable disease.[13]

Within two months, the secretary of the Department of

Health and Human Services had removed HIV from the list of sicknesses that can keep someone from entering the country.[14] The Bush administration then proposed formal rule changes designed to lift the rules prohibiting foreigners with AIDS or certain other diseases from entering the United States. In doing so, the administration noted that the "risk of . . . HIV infection comes not from the nationality of the infected person, but from the specific behaviors that are practiced" and that the new policy would "bring us in line with the best medical thinking."[15] News reports noted that "[v]irtually all leading medical authorities had condemned the ban on HIV-infected people as based on prejudice rather than on sound public policy."[16]

However, just a week before the proposed rule changes would have gone into effect, the Bush administration indicated that it was seriously considering a reversal. News reports attributed the possible change to pressure from conservatives, with more than 39,000 protest letters having been generated.[17] One congressman called the reversal "just some raw meat that George Bush can throw to Republican primitives."[18] As the deadline neared, the secretary of the Department of HHS and the assistant secretary for Health were both reportedly still supporting the change.[19] Within a matter of days and just before the effective date of the proposed rule changes, the Bush administration said it had indefinitely postponed any such change.[20]

The final decision came at the beginning of August 1991.[21] Within two weeks, Harvard University canceled the International AIDS Conference, which it would have hosted in Boston in 1992.[22] The Harvard AIDS Institute indicated that broad participation by people with HIV, health professionals, and other essential participants has been the key to success of the several previous international AIDS conferences and observed that it was not then possible to assure that U.S. immigration policy would allow such broad participation at the 1992 conference.[23]

NOTES

1. See generally 5 C. Gordon & H. Rosenfeld, *Immigration Law and Procedure* 25–9 *et seq.* (1987).

2. INA Section 212(a)(6), codified at 8 U.S.C. Section 1182(a)(6).

3. 52 Fed. Reg. 109, 21,532–33, amending 42 C.F.R. Section 34.2(8).

4. 42 C.F.R. Section 34.2.

5. Pub. L. 100–71.

6. See Section 518.

7. See generally Chapter 17, "Immigration," *AIDS: The Legal Issues, Discussion Draft of the American Bar Association AIDS Coordinating Committee*, 1988, p. 239.

8. "Foreigners with AIDS to Be Permitted Limited Entry to U.S.," *The Washington Post*, May 19, 1989, p. A20.

9. See *AIDS Update*, Lambda Legal Defense and Education Fund, Inc., Vol. 3, No. 7 (April/May 1989), pp. 5–6.

10. "U.S. Won't End AIDS Immigration Ban," a New York Times story appearing in the *Fort Lauderdale Sun-Sentinel*, May 26, 1991, p. 3A.

11. "Bush Relaxes U.S. Policies on AIDS Visas," an Associated Press story appearing in the *Fort Lauderdale Sun-Sentinel*, April 14, 1990, p. 3A. See also "Special 10-Day Visa Aims to Save AIDS Conference," a Los Angeles Times Service story appearing in *The Miami Herald*, April 14, 1990, p. 3A.

12. Opinion Letter No. B–239598, Comptroller General of the United States, May 17, 1990. See *AIDS Lit. Rptr.*, June 8, 1990, p. 4609.

13. "New Law Overhauls Quotas," a Sun-Sentinel wire services story appearing in the *Fort Lauderdale Sun-Sentinel*, November 30, 1990, p. 3A.

14. "AIDS-Virus Infection No Longer to Bar Entry to U.S., Officials Say," a New York Times Service story appearing in *The Miami Herald*, January 4, 1991, p. 1A.

15. "U.S. to Lift AIDS, VD Immigration Ban," an Associated Press story appearing in *The Miami Herald*, January 26, 1991, p. 9A.

16. "U.S. Expected to Lift AIDS Travelers' Ban," a San Fran-

cisco Chronicle story appearing in the *Fort Lauderdale Sun-Sentinel,* January 26, 1991, p. 3A.

17. See n. 10, *supra.*

18. *Id.*

19. "Health Officials Pan Reversal of AIDS Immigration Policy," *The Miami Herald,* May 28, 1991, p. 14A.

20. "Immigration Ban on HIV Carriers Stands, U.S. Says," *The Miami Herald,* May 30, 1991, p. 1A.

21. "U.S. Keeps Ban on Immigrants Carrying HIV," a Washington Post Service story appearing in *The Miami Herald,* August 2, 1991, p. 13A.

22. "Harvard Cancels Boston AIDS Conference," a Reuters story appearing in the *Fort Lauderdale Sun-Sentinel,* August 17, 1991, p. 9A.

23. *Id.*

13

Insurance

Much of the early focus of AIDS-related legal issues was on such prominent issues as education and employment. Insurance occupied a less visible role, but its importance quickly became apparent. As the insurance industry grew increasingly aware of the financial consequences of this new AIDS phenomenon, it sought ways to escape from responsibility for health-care costs; as affected populations and political decision-makers became increasingly aware of the potential for costs that neither was prepared to bear, insurance soared in importance as a legal issue.

In the earliest stages of the AIDS chronology, insurers rather freely admitted to trying to screen out applications from single men in the nation's largest cities, as approximately 80% of the AIDS cases at that time occurred in this group.[1] They were also certainly denying life insurance coverage to those already diagnosed with AIDS. Denying coverage to those already diagnosed with a preexisting condition that was then considered to be a terminal illness is, of course, a different thing from denying coverage to those who were considered at high risk for the disease. The insurers, however, seemed unable—or unwilling—to see the difference.

Since those early days, the insurance industry's practices relating to HIV disease have come under increasing government regulation. Although one group of officials related to the insurance industry has acted with logic and compassion, most insurers have generally acted out of pocketbook protection, and some have been widely criticized for failure to consider what many regard as fairness or the underlying principles on which insurance is supposed to be based.

First, let us look at some of the early abuses. In April 1987, there were reports of an administrative complaint in Texas against a company that had refused to sell a single man life insurance because he had named a same-gender roommate as beneficiary.[2]

At about the same time, suit was filed in New York against an insurer that allegedly tested an applicant's blood for HIV antibodies without the applicant's consent. This suit asserted particularly egregious conduct in that after the blood had tested positive for HIV antibodies, the company's staff had allegedly informed the applicant's insurance agent and others of the positive result, stating further that the test confirmed that the applicant was gay. The staff also reportedly reproduced and used the application during agent training sessions without any attempt to conceal the applicant's identity.[3]

Another example of such abuse occurred in the summer of 1987 when the California Department of Insurance had to order an insurer to process an application for life insurance without requiring HIV-antibody testing.[4]

Also in California, an insurer was charged with "redlining," a practice whereby a geographic territory is carved out and its residents excluded from consideration for coverage simply by virtue of their addresses. According to a former employee of the insurer, applications from the redlined district were stored so as to give the appearance that medical histories were being checked and then rejection letters sent out implying that the medical histories had disqualified the applicants. The district redlined was the San Francisco area with its heavily gay population.[5]

California and several of its political subdivisions have especially strong civil rights protections that extend traditional civil rights laws to cover discrimination on the basis of sexual orientation. And sexual orientation, so far as it can be ascertained or even best-guessed, has been the persistent basis of complaints about insurance industry discrimination. One such suit arose when an insurance applicant refused to answer a supplemental questionnaire and was, therefore, denied health insurance coverage. The questionnaire was being required only from single males who fit a certain profile, which included "antique dealers, interior decorators, florists, restaurant employees, consultants, and people in the jewelry and fashion businesses."[6]

Questions as to whether applicants have already tested positive for HIV antibodies have repeatedly been the subject of suits. As early as the end of 1987, the laws of three states and the District of Columbia and the insurance departments in seven other states prohibited or proposed to prohibit application questions about previous HIV-antibody test results.[7] Since then, the positions of most jurisdictions have been refined as increasing thought has been given to this issue.

Some jurisdictions also prohibit the actual testing of insurance applicants for HIV antibodies, a step well beyond prohibiting the asking for HIV-antibody test history. The District of Columbia was among these jurisdictions,[8] and the law prompted resolutions of disapproval in both houses of the Congress. When the congressional resolutions of disapproval did not pass, the insurance industry challenged the law in court. The D.C. act was ruled constitutional,[9] but any long-term impact of the provision was lost when the law was repealed in a larger power struggle between the D.C. government and the Congress on somewhat related issues of lesbian and gay rights.

The way for much of the responsible and sensible direction being taken on AIDS and insurance issues nationally was paved by the National Association of Insurance Commis-

sioners (NAIC), which in December of 1986 adopted guidelines recommended by its Advisory Committee on AIDS.[10]
Those guidelines include the prohibition of discrimination on
the basis of sexual orientation. NAIC, however, is merely an
association of state insurance regulators, and it has no authority to issue actual regulations in any jurisdiction. Though
NAIC's opinion is certainly weighty, it is still up to each jurisdiction's insurance department or legislature to actually
adopt and implement any such proposals.

In spite of the NAIC guidelines, 86% of commercial insurers were still trying to identify applicants who have been
infected with HIV, according to a March 1988 report of the
congressional Office of Technology Assessment. Approximately half of the 61 companies responding to the survey
reported that they routinely required some applicants, usually men, to undergo HIV-antibody testing. Almost one-third
considered sexual orientation as a factor in underwriting decisions.[11]

One jurisdiction that has adopted what this author con-
siders to be a thoughtful and reasonable approach is Florida.
It did so as a part of its comprehensive AIDS legislation. Insurers are allowed to test for HIV or a related medical condition only if the test is based on the applicant's medical history or current medical condition or is required of all persons
in the same risk class applying for the same threshold coverage limits. Sexual orientation cannot be used to identify a
risk class or otherwise determine who gets tested. Insurers
may inquire as to whether an applicant has ever tested HIV-
positive or been diagnosed with AIDS, ARC, or a related
medical condition, but insurers may not inquire whether an
applicant has ever been tested for HIV antibodies. The difference is a fine line to some, but it is logical and important:
the permissible inquiry goes toward establishing a preexisting medical condition for which an insurer should not have
to take responsibility in a new policy; the impermissible inquiry would go only toward stereotyping and discrimination
and would deter people from seeking testing. Florida also
generally prohibits testing without prior informed consent
and prohibits group health coverage exclusions or limitations

of coverage of HIV-related expenses, subject to a total benefits limit.[12]

Despite these early abuses and the progress made under NAIC's leadership and otherwise since then, insurers persist in attempting to protect their financial well-being, certainly an understandable posture. "Insurance companies . . . across the country are using unfair and 'devious' tactics to avoid paying claims for AIDS-related medical problems, according to lawyers and others who work with AIDS patients . . . 'It's definitely happening, and they're very creative about how they do it,'" said a research planner with the Health Council of South Florida. "[L]awsuits in which AIDS patients claim that either insurers or employers have discriminated against them are becoming more common as the AIDS epidemic expands."[13]

For example, suits are still being filed about insurers testing without the applicant's consent. In late 1988, suit was filed in Massachusetts against an insurer that allegedly performed an HIV-antibody test on an applicant's blood after a specific promise not to do so.[14]

Several state insurance regulators have attempted to regulate the use of HIV-antibody testing in underwriting decisions, and at least two have had their efforts in that regard cut short by the courts. A New York trial court invalidated that state's insurance department's regulations prohibiting HIV-antibody testing for health insurance applicants. The court said that the New York superintendent of insurance lacked the authority to issue such a measure.[15] The state's highest court later agreed with that finding.[16]

Just seven months later, the Supreme Judicial Court of Massachusetts overturned a lower court decision and struck down regulations prohibiting HIV-antibody testing for health insurance purposes, also on the grounds that the state commissioner of insurance lacked the authority to issue regulations to that effect without legislative direction on the issue.[17]

On at least one occasion, an insurer has simply refused to pay for no apparent legal reason. Suit was filed in California by a man who had bought a policy specially designed for persons considered at high risk for AIDS. The policy was sold as a supplement to other insurance and promised to pay only if AIDS was diagnosed at least 90 days after the effective date of the policy. The insured's diagnosis came four months after the effective date, and the insurer claimed that it was therefore a preexisting condition.[18]

Other cases too have focused on the possibility of a preexisting condition, sometimes finding that one did indeed exist and therefore denying coverage. A federal court sitting in Oregon ruled in 1990 that an insurer was entitled to cancel a disability insurance policy for which the HIV-positive insured had applied on the same day but after learning that he had Kaposi's Sarcoma, a skin cancer that is one of the classic HIV-related opportunistic infections.[19]

Somewhat similarly, a federal court declared invalid a life insurance policy on an insured who contracted an HIV-associated opportunistic infection after the policy had lapsed for nonpayment of premiums but before the insured made the application for reinstatement.[20]

And a federal appeals court ruled that a $50,000 life insurance policy issued to an insured who subsequently died of AIDS was never valid because of the insured's failure to disclose a cigarette habit where the application had asked for such information.[21]

But the Supreme Court of Kansas ruled that a man's failure to tell a prospective insurer that he had already tested HIV-positive did not constitute fraud where the application contained no question related to AIDS.[22] "It was the insurance company's responsibility to ask the questions to which it wanted answers," the court said.[23]

And a state court did require the insurer to pay according to the terms of a life insurance policy that the insurer claimed had been incorrectly processed by one of its agents. The insured, a priest, died from AIDS within two months, but at the time of the application, he was in good health and truthfully answered the only questions asked by the agent. The agent held the application briefly before submitting it, and the insured was already sick by the time the application was approved.[24]

A question that often arises in such preexisting condition cases is whether the insured knew of the condition. An appellate federal court found for the insured in a case where he had attested to a lack of awareness of any pertinent ailment to the best of his knowledge and belief at the time of the application and where both sides had conceded such lack of knowledge of the condition that did, in fact, already exist.[25]

One of the most interesting of the preexisting condition cases involves an allegation that the insured fraudulently completed a statement of good health and had an HIV-free imposter take the required blood test in conjunction with the policy application. The insurer asked a federal court in New York to relieve it from paying the $1.9 million death benefit.[26] The estate of the deceased insured not only denied all allegations of fraud, but it filed its own suit in Florida state courts seeking to force the insurance company to pay the claim.[27]

In what is probably the most blatantly fraudulent of the preexisting condition cases, a North Dakota insurance agent made himself the beneficiary of $285,000 in life insurance he sold his son after the son had already been diagnosed with AIDS. He also made himself the beneficiary of $35,000 in life insurance he sold to a man with AIDS who was caring for the agent's son. It was clear that he had lied on both applications about the health status of the "applicants." He was fined $10,000 by the state insurance commission in April 1991 and was barred from selling insurance. The state insurance commissioner said that the agent "apparently saw his son's lingering demise due to AIDS as a business opportunity" and called the incident "the most morally bankrupt act of an agent I've ever seen."[28]

Another objection sometimes being raised by insurers is that the treatments performed or being sought are experimental, and many health policies do not cover experimental treatments. In one case on this issue, a New York court rejected the insurer's claim that a bone marrow transplant was experimental and ordered the insurer to cover the expected $150,000 cost. The transplant was to be from the patient's identical twin brother.[29]

And there is still a string of cases appearing in which discrimination is the issue. Applicants living in urban areas were the target in a New Jersey case in which the state insurance department cited an insurer with violating guidelines then in effect. Only applicants in certain zip codes seeking life insurance coverage in excess of $100,000 were required to take HIV-antibody tests.[30]

More often, though, the discrimination has focused on sexual orientation. Several cases are particularly interesting. Suit was filed in 1988 by a 26-year-old unmarried heterosexual male who lived in the Greenwich Village area of New York City with a male roommate against an insurer that had refused to sell him life insurance. The suit alleged that the denial was based on the mistaken conclusion that the applicant was gay.[31] The case was settled without any admission of wrongdoing by the insurer.[32]

Another such case resulted from the settlement of the "supplemental questionnaire" case noted above, the case that arose because the insurer asked only single males who fit that certain profile (antique dealers, interior decorators, florists).[33] The case was resolved by a private settlement in which the insurer agreed not to discriminate against applicants on the basis of sexual orientation or to attempt to determine applicants' sexual orientation or to weed out those who may be at high risk for HIV disease.[34] Just days after that settlement, however, the insurer announced cancellation of group insurance policies covering approximately 14,000 Californians. Multiple suits were filed in response.[35]

And in a most interesting development, the Oregon Civil Rights Division issued a preliminary ruling that an employer's exclusion of AIDS-related treatments from the company's health insurance coverage was discrimination based not on sexual orientation but on sex.[36] The early 1988 ruling was keyed to the disparate impact with which HIV disease was then found among males. This was the first such ruling based on sex—not sexual orientation—discrimination. The use of this theory is probably not likely to be attempted elsewhere, now that HIV disease is showing alarming infection rates in women.

While the issue seemed more one of intrusion into irrelevant matters than outright discrimination on the basis of sexual orientation, one can nevertheless see overtones of apparent sexual orientation issues in a case in which an insurer attempted to force an applicant to respond to questions about his specific sexual practices and partners.[37]

And there is increasing attention to the practice of employers trying to limit their expenses by changing their coverages from outside insurers to self-insured plans, especially once one or more employees files HIV-related expense claims. Self-insured plans are allowed under the federal Employee Retirement Income Security Act, known as ERISA.[38] Because they are authorized by federal law, these plans generally escape regulation by state laws and the jurisdiction of state insurance commissioners. And the laws and regulations these plans escape are often those most heavily relied on by employees with HIV disease.

In one of the first of these cases, a Florida man filed employment discrimination charges against his employer. After the employee had already been diagnosed with AIDS, the employer changed from a medical plan with a lifetime cap of $1 million to one with a $15,000 lifetime benefit for AIDS-related expenses. In late 1989, however, the Florida Commission on Human Relations found that the employer had articulated and substantiated legitimate, nondiscriminatory reasons for the change of insurance plans and that the complaining employee had not shown those reasons to be pretextual excuses to mask unlawful discrimination.[39]

A much better known case arose in Texas, where an employer had changed plans from an outside one to a self-insured plan after the employee with HIV disease revealed his illness to company officials.[40] The change of insurance plans meant that the cap on AIDS-related benefits went from $1 million to $5,000. The court found that the change was not unlawfully discriminatory.[41]

In a similar case, a different federal court rejected a request from a man with an advanced case of AIDS for a mandatory restraining order to require the man's former employer to continue coverage of his medical expenses even though the employer had changed benefits plans and capped payments for AIDS at $25,000.[42]

In a case not related to HIV disease, the U.S. Supreme Court held that ERISA did preempt a provision of state law,[43] and many analysts of AIDS legal issues saw clear and negative implications for challenges by former and present employees to employers' changes to ERISA plans with lower HIV-disease benefit caps than had been afforded before the changes.

Seemingly notwithstanding the Supreme Court ruling, an Indiana Civil Rights Commission hearing officer recommended two weeks later that a food service be found in violation of the state's civil rights laws and be forced to revise its self-insurance employee benefits plan that capped lifetime benefits for AIDS at $50,000 while limiting payments for most other illnesses to $1 million. The hearing officer said that ERISA does not supersede state civil rights laws as ERISA was instituted to promote uniformity among states regarding workers' benefits and that the state law in question furthers a nondiscriminatory policy established under other federal laws.[44]

A *Washington Post* analysis of the issue summarized it well. "Many of the nation's employers, looking for ways to cut the cost of health insurance for their workers, have taken on the job themselves. Instead of buying a policy from an insurance company, the employer pays out of its own pocket. It may hire an insurer to process the paper work, but otherwise it functions as if it were the employees' insurance company," the analysis explained. "This self-insurance not only spares the employer from paying the insurance company's profit, but under federal law it also exempts the employer from state and local requirements that may increase the costs of the coverage. Employers turn to self-insurance to avoid having to provide [some] state-required benefits . . . But now a small number of employers are trying to use self-insurance to escape the cost of something else: AIDS. Arguing that federal law overrides state antidiscrimination laws . . . employers are switching to self-insurance and then capping benefits for AIDS and related ailments at a fraction of what is allowed for other physical illnesses."[45]

Even under ERISA, though, there are certain consumer rights that can't be overcome. For example, a federal court in the District of Columbia ruled that there was no liability for an insurer that failed to advise an insured of his right to convert his insurance coverage to an individual policy when the employer company was being sold.[46] But that ruling was reversed, the appellate court finding that the insurer had an affirmative duty upon inquiry, which was in fact made, to convey to a lay beneficiary correct and complete information about his status and options when the group policy was canceled.[47]

NOTES

1. "Study Finds Most Health Insurers Screen Applicants for AIDS Virus," *The New York Times*, February 18, 1988, p. A1.

2. See *AIDS Update*, Lambda Legal Defense and Education Fund, Inc., No. 17 (April 1987), p. 4.

3. *Doe v. Prudential Insurance Co.*, S.D.N.Y., No. 87-Civ. 2040, filed March 26, 1987.

4. See *AIDS Update*, Lambda Legal Defense and Education Fund, Inc., Vol. 2, No. 1 (June/July 1987), p. 4.

5. See *AIDS Update*, Lambda Legal Defense and Education Fund, Inc., No. 13 (December 1986), pp. 5-6.

6. See *AIDS Update*, Lambda Legal Defense and Education Fund, Inc., No. 10 (September 1986), p. 5.

7. See Terl, Allan H., "Emerging Issues of AIDS and Insurance," 12 Nova L. Rev. 1291, 1293 (Spring 1988).

8. D.C. Act 6-170.

9. *American Council of Life Ins. v. District of Columbia*, 645 F.Supp. 84 (D.D.C. 1986).

10. See *AIDS Update*, Lambda Legal Defense and Education Fund, Inc., No. 12 (November 1986), pp. 8-9, and No. 13 (December 1986), p. 8.

11. See *AIDS Update*, Lambda Legal Defense and Education Fund, Inc., Vol. 2, No. 6 (March 1988), pp. 4-5.

12. Section 627.429, Florida Statutes (1989).

13. "Insurers Evade AIDS Claims, Patients Say," *Palm Beach Post*, April 23, 1990, p. 1A.

14. *Doe v. Connecticut Mutual Life Insurance Co.*, MA Super. Ct., Suffolk Cty., No. 88-6543-C, November 17, 1988. See *AIDS Update*, Lambda Legal Defense and Education Fund, Inc., Vol. 3, No. 4 (December 1988), p. 7.

15. See *AIDS Update*, Lambda Legal Defense and Education Fund, Inc., Vol. 2, No. 8 (May 1988), p. 5.

16. *Health Association of America v. Corcoran*, NY Ct. of App., No. 90/282. See *AIDS Lit. Rptr.*, December 28, 1990, p. 5531.

17. *Life Insurance Association of Massachusetts et al. v. Commissioner of Insurance*, MA Sup. Jud. Ct., No. 87-5321, November 16, 1988. See *AIDS Update*, Lambda Legal Defense and Education Fund, Inc., Vol. 3, No. 4 (December 1988), p. 6.

18. *Franz v. Coastal Insurance Co.*, CA Super. Ct., San Francisco Cty., No. 880812, filed August 31, 1987. See *AIDS Update*, Lambda Legal Defense and Education Fund, Inc., Vol. 2, No. 5 (February 1988), p. 3.

19. *Elder v. SMA Life Assurance Co.*, D. Ore., No. 88-1261-FR. See *AIDS Lit. Rptr.*, May 25, 1990, p. 4547.

20. *Connecticut Mutual Life Insurance Co. v. Gastman*, D. Md., No. HAR-89-1629. See *AIDS Lit. Rptr.*, January 11, 1991, p. 5620.

21. *New York Life Insurance Co. v. Johnson et al.*, 3rd Cir., No. 90-1406. See *AIDS Lit. Rptr.*, January 25, 1991, p. 5696.

22. *The Advocate*, No. 577 (May 21, 1991), p. 27.

23. *Estate of Maurice Behnke v. Reserve Life Insurance Co.*, KS Sup. Ct., No. 65,486. See *AIDS Lit. Rptr.*, May 10, 1991, p. 6252.

24. *Jackson National Life Insurance Co. v. Receconi et al.*, NM Dist. Ct., Sante Fe Cty., No. SF 88-532[C]. See *AIDS Lit. Rptr.*, October 12, 1990, p. 5161.

25. *William Penn Life Insurance Co. of New York v. Sands*, 11th Cir., No. 89-6017. See *AIDS Lit. Rptr.*, October 12, 1990, p. 5163.

26. *Massachusetts General Life Insurance Co. v. Fioretti*, S.D.N.Y., No. 90 CIV.3726. See *AIDS Lit. Rptr.*, August 24, 1990, p. 4960, and "Insurance Refuses to Pay AIDS Claim," *Fort Lauderdale Sun-Sentinel*, July 7, 1990, p. 4B.

27. *Fioretti v. Massachusetts General Life Insurance Co.*, FL Cir. Ct., Broward Cty., No. 90-16963; S.D. Fla., No. 90-6530. See *AIDS Lit. Rptr.*, September 14, 1990, p. 5030.

28. *The Advocate*, Issue No. 578 (June 4, 1991), p. 27.

29. *Bradley v. Empire Blue Cross and Blue Shield,* NY Sup. Ct., N.Y. Cty., No. 15290/90. See *AIDS Lit. Rptr.,* August 10, 1990, p. 4903, and "Insurer Must Pay for Marrow Transplant," *The Miami Herald,* August 2, 1990, p. 15A.

30. *In the Matter of Midland National Life Insurance Co.,* NJ Dept. of Insurance, Order to Show Cause No. 90–19. See *AIDS Lit. Rptr.,* December 28, 1990, p. 5541.

31. *Doe v. United Services Life Insurance Co.,* NY Sup. Ct., N.Y. Cty., No. 88 Civ. 5630 (RWS), July 28, 1988. See *AIDS Update,* Lambda Legal Defense and Education Fund, Inc., Vol. 3, No. 3 (November 1988), p. 3.

32. *Id.* See *AIDS Update,* Lambda Legal Defense and Education Fund, Inc., Vol. 3, No. 11 (September/October 1989), p. 7.

33. See n. 6, *supra.*

34. *National Gay Rights Advocates et al. v. Great Republic Insurance Co. et al.,* CA Super. Ct., San Francisco Cty., No. 857323. See *AIDS Lit. Rptr.,* May 25, 1990, p. 4548.

35. *Rosco v. Great Republic,* No. 919372, *White v. Great Republic,* No. 919933, CA Super. Ct., San Francisco Cty. See *AIDS Lit. Rptr.,* July 13, 1990, p. 4752.

36. *In the Matter of Beaverton Nissan and M.F. Saltla, Inc.,* Oregon Civil Rights Division, Case No. ST–EM–HP–870108–1353. See *AIDS Update,* Lambda Legal Defense and Education Fund, Inc., Vol. 2, No. 6 (March 1988), p. 5.

37. *Guardian Life Ins. Co. v. Smyth,* NY Sup. Ct., N.Y. Cty., Index No. 07900/87, July 22, 1988. See *AIDS Update,* Lambda Legal Defense and Education Fund, Inc., Vol. 3, No. 1 (September 1988), pp. 6–7.

38. Pub. L. 93–406, as amended.

39. *Starkey v. Arvida,* FL Comm. on Human Rel., FCHR No. 88–3936, Determination filed November 22, 1989. See *AIDS Update,* Lambda Legal Defense and Education Fund, Vol. 2, No. 10 (July 1988), pp. 3–4.

40. *McGann v. H&H Music Co. et al.,* S.D. Tex., Houston Div., No. H–89–1995. See *AIDS Update,* Lambda Legal Defense and Education Fund, Inc., Vol. 3, No. 10 (August 1989), pp. 2–3.

41. *Id.* See *AIDS Lit. Rptr.,* August 10, 1990, p. 4898.

42. *Owens v. Storehouse, Inc. et al.,* N.D. Ga., Atlanta Div., No. 1:90–CV–2292–JOF. See *AIDS Lit. Rptr.,* November 23, 1990, p. 5406, and *AIDS Update,* Lambda Legal Defense and Education Fund, Inc., Vol. 4, No. 2 (December 1990), p. 5.

43. *FMC Corp. v. Holliday,* U.S. Sup. Ct., No. 89–1048. See

AIDS Lit. Rptr., January 11, 1991, p. 5629, and *AIDS Update,* Lambda Legal Defense and Education Fund, Inc., Vol. 4, No. 2 (December 1990), p. 3.

44. *Westhoven v. Lincoln Foodservice Products, Inc.*, IN Civil Rights Comm., No. EMha89030350. See *AIDS Lit. Rptr.*, December 28, 1990, p. 5537, and *AIDS Update,* Lambda Legal Defense and Education Fund, Inc., Vol. 4, No. 2 (December 1990), p. 4.

45. "Employers Try to Cut AIDS Costs by Self-Insurance," a Washington Post story appearing in the Weekly Business Section of the *Fort Lauderdale Sun-Sentinel,* January 21, 1991, p. 4.

46. *Eddy et al. v. Colonial Life Insurance Co. of America,* D.D.C., No. 88–1038. See *AIDS Lit. Rptr.*, September 22, 1989, p. 3362.

47. *Id.,* D.C. Cir., No. 89–7206. See *AIDS Lit. Rptr.*, December 28, 1990, p. 5532, and *AIDS Update,* Lambda Legal Defense and Education Fund, Inc., Vol. 4, No. 2 (December 1990), p. 4.

14

Military

Military law is another specialty area with which only a comparatively small segment of the population comes into contact. Nevertheless, a cursory examination of AIDS-related developments in military law can give a flavor of how this traditionally conservative American institution, as compared to the civilian sector, has approached the subject of HIV disease.

The first noted case of public action on HIV issues occurred in May 1987 when an Army investigator in Arizona recommended that an enlisted man be court-martialed for having had unprotected sex with three enlisted personnel even though the man knew that he was HIV-positive.[1] One wonders whether the military's actions were entirely motivated by the unsafe character of the sexual activity or by the man's choice of sex partners, identified respectively in the reports on the case as "Patricia," "Jane Doe," and "Anthony."

In June 1988, an administrative board in Florida found that the removal of an HIV-positive but asymptomatic man from active duty was improper[2]—a most progressive ruling for that early in the AIDS chronology. That case has gone on to federal court.

In 1989, the U.S. Court of Military Appeals rejected an appeal by an HIV-positive officer who was penalized for having had unprotected sex with a soldier of the opposite sex who was unaware of the officer's HIV infection and who had since tested positive for HIV antibodies.[3] One should note, however, that unprotected sex by one who is infected with HIV and who fails to warn the sexual partner is a criminal act in many states under civilian law.

In June 1990, the U.S. Court of Appeals affirmed a lower federal court's dismissal of a Naval reservist's claim that his release from temporary active duty after being diagnosed HIV-positive violated the Rehabilitation Act. The courts' rulings found a "military exception" that meant the terms of the Rehabilitation Act did not apply to the uniformed services.[4] Pursuant to a change made in Defense Department regulations in April 1987—after the underlying act had already occurred in this case—active duty status is prohibited for HIV-positive Naval Reserve personnel.[5]

And in October 1990, the U.S. Supreme Court let stand two other lower court decisions. The first involved a 1988 "safe sex" order and an HIV-positive enlisted man's conviction on charges of willful disobedience and aggravated assault for having had sex with a civilian woman without informing her of his HIV infection or preventing the exchange of bodily fluids. The soldier had pled guilty to the charges during a general court-martial and had been stripped of pay, imprisoned for two years, and given an honorable discharge. He argued in the appeal that the order was overly broad and beyond the reach of the military.[6]

The other case questioned the constitutionality of a dishonorable discharge and a six-year prison sentence for aggravated assault given to a former Air Force sergeant as a result of a homosexual encounter that included unprotected sex with a partner unaware of the sergeant's HIV-positive condition.[7]

The military's special status outside the coverage of

many civilian laws, including the Rehabilitation Act and other civil rights acts protecting the handicapped from discrimination, will surely generate even more attention to HIV-related legal issues. And the popular association of HIV disease with gay sex, coupled with the military's fierce opposition to allowing homosexuals within its ranks, will keep these cases within the focus of civil rights activists.

NOTES

1. See *AIDS Update,* Lambda Legal Defense and Education Fund, Inc., No. 18 (May 1987), p. 8. The HIV-antibody test results were ultimately held to be inadmissible as evidence. See *AIDS Update,* Vol. 2, No. 3 (October 1987), p. 6.

2. *Doe v. Lehman,* M.D. Fla, No. 86–971–Civ–J–16, March 15, 1988.

3. *U.S. v. Womack,* 29 Mil. Just. Rept. 88 (U.S. Ct. of Military App., September 29, 1989).

4. *Doe v. Garrett,* 11th Cir., No. 89–3404. See *AIDS Lit. Rptr.,* July 13, 1990, p. 4742. Review denied by the U.S. Supreme Court, U.S. Sup. Ct., No. 90–803. See *AIDS Lit. Rptr.,* March 22, 1991, p. 5995.

5. See *AIDS Lit. Rptr.,* July 13, 1990, p. 4743.

6. *Dumford v. United States,* U.S. Sup. Ct., No. 90–204. See *AIDS Lit. Rptr.,* October 12, 1990, p. 5164.

7. *Johnson v. United States,* U.S. Sup. Ct., No. 90–61. See *AIDS Lit. Rptr.,* October 26, 1990, p. 5243.

15

Prisons

Prison law must be seen, like the military and immigration, as another highly specialized area to which traditional legal reasoning might not always apply. In looking at how prisons are administered, one must bear in mind frequent and very real conditions of overcrowding, violence, underfunded medical care, and correctional officers' understandable fears of disease transmission from very untraditional kinds of contact. It should not surprise, other than the most naive observers, that prisoner-correctional officer contact may include spitting or the throwing of urine or feces and that correctional officers must be mindful of these situations at all times. The possibility of becoming infected with HIV is an additional problem that prison officials must include in their reasons for exercising constant caution.

Still, these pressures cannot justify or excuse some of the treatment prison staff and other prisoners have given to those with AIDS, to those with asymptomatic HIV infection, or to those merely suspected of having the virus. There are countless stories of cold food being pushed under cell doors;

of guards using masks and gloves to escort prisoners, thus
revealing to other, potentially hostile prisoners one's HIV
positivity; of HIV-positive prisoners being locked up in medical isolation cells with no exercise, no visitors, no jobs, even
no right to seal their own mail.

Some guards have resorted to the use of "moon suits," so
called because of their similar appearance to those worn by
astronauts, to protect themselves; inmates have threatened
to riot if those with the virus were integrated into the general prison housing; inmates have filed suit to seek mandatory testing of all inmates and isolation of those found to
carry the virus; and one HIV-positive inmate was reportedly
even subjected to having his cell torched by other inmates
seeking to have him removed from the general prisoner population.

One of the first issues confronted is testing of inmates for
HIV. In mid-1988, California initiated anonymous HIV-
antibody testing of all new prisoners to ascertain the scope
of infection within the prison population.[1] In a 1990 decision
considered very significant by AIDS-law watchers, a federal
court affirmed the right of the Alabama Department of Corrections to conduct mandatory testing of inmates as well as
to segregate those found to have HIV-related infections.[2]

But the U.S. Court of Appeals for the 9th Circuit, generally considered rather progressive on most issues, unanimously reversed and sent back to the lower court that lower
court's opinion upholding the constitutionality of a mandatory blood-testing program for all Nevada Corrections Department inmates.[3] This issue is, thus, far from being resolved conclusively.

Next come the cases dealing with separation of HIV-
infected inmates from the rest of the prison population. In
mid-1988, inmates at a facility that had been set aside exclusively to house HIV-positive prisoners sued, alleging gross
overcrowding and consequent severe emotional and psychological problems.[4] In October 1988, a New York court issued a
preliminary injunction after finding that placement of HIV-
positive inmates in a segregated dormitory violated their
constitutional right to privacy.[5]

In Connecticut, a consent judgment—a settlement agreement between the parties approved by the court—provided that HIV-positive inmates would no longer be segregated from other prisoners solely on the basis of their HIV status.[6] The suit, including all aspects of its resolution even by agreement of the parties, went on for some two years, with the final terms including health-related requirements for intake and assessment of incoming inmates, delivery of routine care for infected inmates, access to medical care for acute illnesses, drug treatment, diet, mental health, dental and vision care, and special treatment for infected female prisoners.[7]

Isolation from the prison population was the indirect issue in the case of an activist arrested during a demonstration protesting inadequate funding for AIDS. He was placed in a cell far-removed from officers on duty. The officers were aware that he had AIDS, and the inmate suffered physical symptoms, which went unattended. He sued for violation of his "due process" rights and discrimination based on the prison system's failure to have in place policies to ensure that persons with AIDS received appropriate treatment while in custody. The claim was initially dismissed in the trial-level federal court, but the U.S. Court of Appeals reinstated the claim.[8]

We have already noted the important Alabama case in which the federal court upheld HIV-infected inmate segregation.[9]

The county prison in Delaware County, Pennsylvania, agreed in May 1991 to end its policy of segregating HIV-infected prisoners to settle a class action suit. The suit had been filed by an inmate subjected to the segregation policy and who, when first diagnosed with HIV infection in 1986, was chained to a bed in a closet that had been converted into an "isolation ward."[10] The prison agreed to abolish its "Special Medical Unit," a 12-bed ward that had held as many as 50 infected inmates; provide AIDS education for staff and inmates; provide confidentiality of medical records; make available pre- and post-test counseling; and provide drug therapy and special services for infected female inmates.[11]

And in a strange twist to the isolation/segregation issue, a federal prison inmate sued the U.S. Bureau of Prisons for $100 billion, alleging negligence and breach of the constitutional right to be free of cruel and unusual punishment because he was, for ten days in 1988, housed with an HIV-positive inmate. The case was dismissed for failure to present facts supporting a finding of constitutional violation and because the public official defendant, sued as an individual, enjoyed a measure of immunity protection from such suits.[12]

The next group of cases involves the issue of confidentiality—privacy as to inmates' status as HIV-positive. In New York, an inmate was found to have a legitimate constitutional claim for wrongful disclosure of his HIV infection to other inmates. The disclosure was the inference easily drawn because he was forced to wear a "hygiene suit,"[13] presumably something akin to the noted moon suit.

A legal action in Washington state resulted in a consent decree in which local jail officials agreed not to reveal an inmate's HIV status to anyone but top prison and medical officials and to conduct training to educate personnel on medical and confidentiality aspects of AIDS.[14]

Fearful that others would learn of his condition, a Florida inmate infected with the AIDS virus refused to take his AZT, a life-prolonging medication, until the prison agreed to dispense it in private. The federal suit alleged that the prison was dispensing AZT multiple times daily in front of other inmates and that staff at the prison had said that the last HIV-infected patient whose condition was made public was viciously assaulted.[15]

AIDS advocacy groups and other groups interested in AIDS issues filed suit in early 1991 challenging the constitutionality of that part of Proposition 96, approved by the voters of California at referendum, requiring that jail officials be given the identities of inmates suffering from HIV-related infections.[16] A request for a preliminary injunction was denied by the trial court, but just four days later, a state appeals court blocked enforcement of the law.[17]

And an anonymous inmate received approval from the

New York Court of Claims to continue his breach of privacy suit against that state based on assertions that corrections personnel there unlawfully gained access to and disseminated his HIV-positive status to persons throughout the prison facility in which he was housed.[18]

Most of these cases allege multiple claims, and one should not assume that these categorizations made here constitute the only grounds on which suit was brought. Most have alleged deprivation of privileges enjoyed by other inmates. Along those lines, a 1989 Texas class action suit alleged that inmates who were otherwise eligible for transfer to a less restrictive pre-parole facility were being denied that opportunity if they were HIV-positive.[19]

Somewhat similarly, allegations of breach of the appropriate standards of medical care resulted in late 1989 in the U.S. Court of Appeals approving the release by a lower court of a prisoner because of the inadequate medical care available to treat his HIV-related illness in the federal prison system.[20] But a three-judge panel of that same appeals court reversed the decision. The panel recognized that the greatest relief to which the prisoner would be entitled would be an injunction against unconstitutionally cruel and unusual punishment so as to bring his medical treatment up to constitutional standards, not release from prison.[21]

And an HIV-positive prisoner at the state penitentiary in Cheyenne, Wyoming, sued corrections officials in June 1991, alleging unconstitutional cruel and unusual punishment in that they denied him treatment to prevent him from progressing to full AIDS.[22]

Some of the issues raised in these cases have seemed a bit unusual, but much of prison-related law simply is unusual. For example, although the New York Supreme Court has recognized the right of inmates to marry subject to somewhat greater restrictions than ordinary citizens,[23] the New York Court of Appeals ruled that a state may deny conjugal visits to prisoners with AIDS, even though such visits are permitted to all other married prisoners.[24] Following a new challenge to the regulations prohibiting the conjugal visits,[25] New York's Corrections Commissioner decided to allow HIV-infected inmates conjugal visits with their spouses, provided that both learn safe-sex practices.[26]

And the persistent issue of HIV disease and food-handling surfaced in this context too. Despite the clear recognition that medical knowledge shows HIV cannot be spread through casual contact involved in food or non-invasive medical services positions, a federal court upheld the constitutionality of federal regulations prohibiting HIV-infected inmates from working in certain food and health services positions within federal prisons. The court cited maintenance of security and avoidance of potentially problematic situations rather than prevention of spread of HIV among the inmate population.[27]

What is perhaps the most bizarre of the prison cases reveals the extraordinary circumstances in which one must view this entire area of law. The case involved a Florida correctional officer who sued the operator of a prison health center laboratory. It was alleged that inadequately supervised inmates working in the lab mixed HIV-tainted blood into the correctional officer's coffee, which he then drank. The case was privately settled with the terms of the settlement not disclosed.[28]

The American Bar Association adopted a policy on AIDS and the criminal justice system in 1989. That policy includes relevant recommendations concerning correctional facilities. The ABA said that appropriately funded training and educational programs regarding HIV should be instituted in all correctional facilities. Further, the ABA recommended that inmates in correctional facilities should be afforded appropriate medical care for the full range of HIV-related infections and should be afforded appropriate counseling as well.

The ABA policy states that prisoners should not be segregated from the general population of the correctional facility or be placed in other special areas solely because of known or perceived HIV status. It specifies that mass HIV-antibody testing should not be done for the purpose of segregating inmates in special cells or areas.

Information about an inmate's HIV status should not be

disclosed except to the warden, key supervisory staff who have a legitimate need for the information, or medical staff for care and treatment purposes, according to the ABA policy.

And the ABA says that parole or temporary release should not be denied a prisoner, nor should a prisoner be barred from participating in other community release programs, solely because of the prisoner's known or perceived HIV status.[29]

The National Commission on AIDS has also addressed these concerns. In March 1991, it issued a report on HIV disease in correctional facilities. The report found that:

- Prisoners with HIV infection are rapidly acquiring tuberculosis and many more are at increased risk from the resurgent tuberculosis epidemic in the nation's prisons.
- Prisoners with HIV are often subject to automatic segregation from the rest of the prison community despite the fact that there is no public health basis for this practice.
- Lack of education of both inmates and staff creates fear and discrimination toward individuals with HIV disease and unjust policies directed toward inmates living with HIV disease.
- Despite high rates of HIV infection and an ideal opportunity for prevention and education efforts, former prisoners are reentering their communities with little or no added knowledge about HIV disease and how to prevent it.[30]

Inmates continue to be tested without their consent, segregated and thus effectively labeled and made subject to other inmates' and staff's ridicule and animosity, and denied privileges available to those not HIV-infected. Perhaps more than any other area of HIV-related law, prison law remains largely inclusive of the results of the fears and ignorance being overcome in other legal areas.

NOTES

1. See *AIDS Update,* Lambda Legal Defense and Education Fund, Inc., Vol. 2, No. 8 (May 1988), p. 7.

2. *Harris v. Thigpen,* M.D. Ala. No. 87V-1109-N, January 8, 1990. See *AIDS Update,* Lambda Legal Defense and Education Fund, Inc., Vol. 4, No. 1 (May 1990), p. 8.

3. *Walker v. Sumner,* 9th Cir., No. 88-15644. See *AIDS Lit. Rptr.,* November 9, 1990, p. 5329.

4. *Gates v. Deukmejian,* E.D. Ca., No. CIVS 87-1636 LKK-JFM, filed January 6, 1988. See *AIDS Update,* Lambda Legal Defense and Education Fund, Inc., Vol. 2, No. 8 (May 1988), p. 7.

5. *Doe v. Coughlin,* 697 F.Supp. 1234 (N.D.N.Y. 1988). See *AIDS Update,* Lambda Legal Defense and Education Fund, Inc., Vol. 3, No. 3 (November 1988), p. 6.

6. *Smith v. Meachum,* D. Conn., Civil No. H-87-221(JAC), 1988.

7. *Doe et al. v. Meachum et al.,* D. Conn., No. H-88562[PCD][JGM]. See *AIDS Lit. Rptr.,* January 25, 1991, p. 5700.

8. *Lind v. City of Philadelphia,* 3rd Cir. No. 89-1778, March 12, 1990. See *AIDS Update,* Lambda Legal Defense and Education Fund, Inc., Vol. 4, No. 2 (July 1990), p. 6.

9. See n. 2, *supra.*

10. *Starkey et al. v. Matty et al.,* E.D Pa., No. 89-9011. See *AIDS Lit. Rptr.,* June 14, 1991, p. 6393.

11. *Id.*

12. *Deutsch v. Federal Bureau of Prisons,* S.D.N.Y., No. 89-CV-3544-RJW. See *AIDS Lit. Rptr.,* June 22, 1990, p. 4694.

13. *Rodriguez v. Coughlin,* W.D.N.Y., No. Civ-87-1577, slip op., June 2, 1989.

14. *Doe v. Clark Cty. et al.,* W.D. Wash., Tacoma, No. C89-460TB. See *AIDS Lit. Rptr.,* October 12, 1990, p. 5166.

15. "Inmate Sues Prison Over Dispensing of AIDS Drug," *Ft. Lauderdale Sun-Sentinel,* August 2, 1990, p. 15A.

16. *Capaldini et al. v. Sheriff of the City and County of San Francisco, Michael Hennessey, et al.,* CA Super. Ct., San Francisco Cty., No. 927822. See *AIDS Lit. Rptr.,* January 25, 1991, p. 5703.

17. See *AIDS Lit. Rptr.,* February 22, 1991, p. 5844.

18. *In the Matter of V. v. State of New York,* NY Ct. of Claims, Albany, Motion M-41290. See *AIDS Lit. Rptr.,* February 22, 1991, p. 5851.

19. *Doe v. Lynaugh,* S.D. Tex., Civil Action No. H–88–2960, filed January 13, 1989. See *AIDS Update,* Lambda Legal Defense and Education Fund, Inc., Vol. 3, No. 7 (April/May 1989), p. 7.

20. *Gomez v. United States,* 725 F.Supp. 526 (S.D. Fla. 1989). See *AIDS Lit. Rptr.,* December 8, 1989, p. 3680.

21. *Gomez v. U.S. Bureau of Prisons,* 899 F.2d 1124 (11th Cir. 1990). See *AIDS Lit. Rptr.,* May 25, 1990, p. 4545, and *AIDS Update,* Lambda Legal Defense and Education Fund, Inc., Vol. 4, No. 2 (December 1990), p. 9.

22. *The Advocate,* No. 582 (July 30, 1991), p. 30.

23. *Turner v. Safley,* 482 U.S. 78 (1987).

24. *Doe v. Coughlin,* 71 N.Y.2d 48 (1987), reconsideration denied, 70 N.Y. 2d (1988).

25. *Zoe et al. v. Coughlin et al.,* N.D. N.Y., No. 91 CV.–0784. See *AIDS Lit. Rptr.,* July 26, 1991, p. 6596.

26. "AIDS Inmates Get Visits," *Fort Lauderdale Sun-Sentinel,* August 6, 1991, p. 3A.

27. *Farmer v. Moritsugu,* W.D. Wis., No. 89–C–926–S. See *AIDS Lit. Rptr.,* May 11, 1990, p. 4461.

28. *Elliot v. Prison Health Services et al.,* FL Cir. Ct., 8th Jud. Cir., No. 87–149CA. See *AIDS Lit. Rptr.,* May 25, 1990, p. 4551.

29. "Policy on AIDS and the Criminal Justice System," American Bar Association, adopted by the House of Delegates, February 7, 1989.

30. Report Number Five: "HIV Disease in Correctional Facilities," National Commission on AIDS, March 1991.

16

Public Accommodations and Professional Regulation

Since the enactment of Title II of the Civil Rights Act of 1964,[1] discrimination on the basis of race, color, religion, and national origin has been unlawful in places of public accommodations. Those old enough will remember the lunch counter sit-ins of the 1950s and '60s as well as separate facilities, such as bathrooms and drinking fountains, for blacks and whites.

The concept of "public accommodations" has traditionally encompassed eating establishments, hotels and motels, and movie theaters and other entertainment facilities. But with the onset of AIDS, there came new cries to extend the concept of public accommodations to a wider variety of professional services not previously considered by many to be within that concept.

Among the first such professional services was the funeral industry. In early 1987, a trial court upheld the right of the New York City Commission on Human Rights to investigate allegations of discrimination against PWAs by funeral homes there.[2] Funeral homes were accused of insisting on

special procedures and the purchase of special burial equipment for HIV-positive bodies, at significantly greater expense than for bodies not so infected. At least one New York
funeral home entered into a settlement agreeing not to require such discriminatory, costly, and unnecessary extras.[3]
And in March 1988, an administrative complaint was filed
against a Connecticut funeral home that refused to embalm
the body of an HIV-positive woman.[4]

Other professions have been affected as well. In June
1987, a California man filed suit against a substance-abuse
treatment program that had dismissed him from its services
because he had tested HIV-positive. The test was a prerequi-
site to which he objected.[5] A year later, a federal court held
that the practice was discriminatory on the basis of handicap
and, therefore, a violation of the 1973 Rehabilitation Act—
the first federal ruling that an asymptomatic HIV-positive
individual was covered by the terms of that nondiscrimination law.[6] The case was settled, with the hospital agreeing to
rescind both its policy of mandatory HIV-antibody testing of
applicants of the drug program and exclusion from the program of persons who are HIV-positive.[7]

One well-known case on this issue involved the refusal of
a Maryland nail salon to serve an HIV-positive woman. The
state's Human Relations Commission declared the refusal to
be a violation of its laws against discrimination by places of
public accommodations.[8]

In April 1989, suit was filed against a California chiropractor who refused service after learning that a potential
patient was HIV-positive. That suit was based on a local ordinance that included a prohibition against discrimination by
businesses. The suit resulted in the issuance of a permanent
injunction against the alleged discrimination, and it was settled for $5,000 in damages the same day the injunction was
issued.[9]

At about the same time as the suit was filed against the
California chiropractor, a New York court granted a temporary restraining order against a nursing-home operator for its
discrimination on the basis of HIV status. An HIV-positive
resident had been isolated from leaving his room and an ad-

jacent hallway area, which meant that physical therapy and showers or baths were made unavailable. This isolation continued for more than a year![10]

Another claim that a nursing home had discriminated on the basis of HIV status in denying an applicant admission was settled, with the terms including payment of monetary damages to the anonymous complainant and a statement that the nursing home "does and shall not discriminate" on the basis of HIV.[11]

And in a nursing-home case compounded by issues of religious freedom, several advocacy groups sued the New York State Health Commissioner for granting, allegedly because of the "institutional conscience," public health law exemptions that would allow nursing homes operated by the Catholic Church to forgo offering otherwise required HIV-prevention education, distribution of condoms, and certain reproductive medical care.[12]

After a major public outcry,[13] a policy of the Arvada, Colorado, volunteer fire department to refuse to respond to calls from people with AIDS and other infectious diseases and instead dispatch a private ambulance was reversed in August 1991.[14]

By far the most interesting of these cases, however, involve medical and dental facilities. Remember that human rights laws in most states already make the denial of the facilities of public accommodations on the basis of handicap unlawful and that AIDS, ARC, and HIV infection have been almost uniformly held to be handicapping conditions within the meaning of those laws. Are then medical and dental facilities public accommodations, meaning that medical and dental service providers may not lawfully deny services on the basis of HIV-positive status? If that is the case, does the prohibition against discrimination extend only to those actually infected with HIV or also to those only perceived as infected?

The first legal tests of these issues apparently came in New York when an administrative law judge (ALJ) said in March 1988 that a dental office was indeed public accommodations under the New York City Administrative Code.[15]

That preliminary ruling was finalized in July 1991 when the ALJ ordered the dentist to pay $7,500 to the estate of the then-deceased complaining patient.[16] The decision came less than two months after the New York City Council approved a measure revising its definition of public accommodations to include private medical offices and thus including them within the coverage of laws that prohibit discrimination by places of public accommodations against persons with HIV.[17]

An ALJ's similarly pro-PWA finding was upheld by the New York City Commission on Human Rights[18] and ultimately by the New York Supreme Court. But in September 1988, in a different New York county, a physician's office was held by the same level court not to be public accommodations within the meaning of the New York antidiscrimination law.[19] That ruling, however, was later reversed by an appellate court, which found that the New York State Division of Human Rights did indeed have authority to decide if the orthopedic doctor's office was a public accommodation and thus subject to the state's human rights law.[20]

As New York struggled with these issues, an ALJ in Illinois ruled in November 1988 that a dental office was a public accommodation under that state's Human Rights Act.[21] The test case resulted in a settlement under the terms of which the accused dentist agreed not to discriminate on the basis of HIV status, not to require HIV-antibody testing of potential patients, and to pay an undisclosed amount of monetary damages.

In a letter ruling in August 1989, the Florida Department of Professional Regulation admonished a dentist for refusing to treat or refer elsewhere a patient who in 1988 disclosed that he was HIV-positive.[22]

And a federal court ruled in late 1990 that the estate of a deceased HIV-positive plaintiff who was refused elective surgery can continue his suit for compensatory damages against the physician and hospital, although its claim for injunctive relief and punitive damages was dismissed.[23] The federal suit was allowed to continue against the hospital because it accepted Medicaid and Medicare; however, a motion to dismiss the suit against the physician, who did not personally accept such federal monies, was granted.[24]

A California suit was settled privately, with the San Francisco-area health clinic defendant agreeing to pay $11,500 in damages and attorneys' fees and to cover the cost of oral surgery required by an HIV-infected patient who claimed to have been denied completion of long-term treatment after a clinic staffer cited a policy against treating persons with HIV-related illnesses.[25]

In May 1991, the New Jersey Public Advocate sued a walk-in dental clinic in that state for its alleged refusal to serve a patient who revealed his HIV-positive status on a screening questionnaire and who was denied service because of that status.[26]

At least one of these cases did not directly involve the medical service provider, but an intermediary. In late 1990, a local human rights agency determined that a physicians' referral service operated from a secretary's home was a place of public accommodations that unlawfully discriminated against an HIV-positive patient in 1988 when it failed to provide him with the names of member physicians who would supply routine and emergency care.[27]

One of the most unusual of the professional regulation cases involved the Illinois Department of Professional Regulation revoking the license of a nurse who was convicted of falsely telling her boyfriend and two other people that they were HIV-positive as a part of a scheme to torment the boyfriend, whom she believed was having an affair with a married woman. The deceit was discovered when the boyfriend took a follow-up HIV-antibody test to confirm the nurse's claim.[28]

Then come the cases involving the denial of professional services to those not necessarily diagnosed as HIV-positive. In November 1989, suit was filed in Hawaii against a dental clinic for refusing to serve a patient. Unlike other cases, the suit in Hawaii alleged discrimination against a patient who was only perceived to be HIV-positive, thus demonstrating all the more clearly the evils of the prejudice that these kinds of legal actions seek to stop or redress.[29] The trial court ruled that the state's public accommodations laws do not protect persons who suffer only perceived discrimination.[30] In April 1991, however, the state's Supreme Court disagreed with that judgment but affirmed the denial of damages on other grounds.[31]

In contrast to the Hawaii case, a New York dental clinic was ordered by a state administrative agency to pay $25,000 in mental-anguish damages to a man who was denied proper treatment for a root canal in 1985 because the dentist perceived that the patient was gay and possibly HIV-infected. The order in the case required future nondiscrimination and education of the clinic's staff as to HIV issues.[32]

A different twist to these cases arose in early 1989 when a dental student sued his school for its refusal to allow him to register because of his HIV-positive status. The student was in his third year of the four-year curriculum. The school contended that the student was not "otherwise qualified" to complete the dental program, as would be required under the terms of the appropriate section of the 1973 Rehabilitation Act.[33]

In examining these cases, one must recognize the hopefully obvious medical implications to those with HIV disease of being unable to get medical or dental treatment as well as the seriousness of the problem. A University of California, San Francisco, survey of 1,045 doctors in residency training nationally found that two-thirds did not plan to treat AIDS patients when they started their practices. Half said they would not want to be known as having people with AIDS among their patients.[34] Some 65% of those surveyed agreed that most IV drug-using patients with AIDS have brought the disease on themselves. Forty-six percent agreed with the same statement when the phrase "gay patients" was substituted, and 35% agreed when "minority patients" was substituted.[35]

The unavailability of dental services has been a particular problem. In a report to the White House and congressional leaders, the National Commission on AIDS said that it "heard repeatedly about a serious shortage of dentists willing to treat people with HIV infection and AIDS . . . [O]ne witness . . . said that the only two dentists in his community who would accept Medicaid declined to see him because he was infected with HIV. . . . One dentist's excuse was that his office was carpeted, and he would not be able to sterilize the room after the visit. The other dentist said she had plants and could not take the risk of him infecting her plants and her plants then infecting her other patients."[36]

In a demonstration of the severity of this problem of obtaining dental services for persons with HIV disease, five persons serving as complainants randomly selected 37 dentists in the greater Philadelphia area with whom appointments were made for dental care. Upon the subsequent revelation that the patient was HIV-positive, 30% of the dentists refused to provide care. Complaints were filed against the 11 dentists for allegedly violating the state Human Relations Act and local Fair Practice Ordinance.[37] Seven of the 11 dentists have sought to have the charges dropped for lack of jurisdiction, claiming that dental offices are not places of public accommodations according to the state's law.[38]

It should be borne in mind that various professional associations—for example, the American Dental Association and state dental associations—have said clearly that there is no reason to discriminate on the basis of HIV status.[39] This seemingly supports the claim that discrimination on the basis of HIV status constitutes a violation of the ethical standards to which most states' licensed professionals are to be held under the terms of their licensure, a potential additional ground for complaint as was used in the Sommers case.[40]

Finally in this regard, some states have legislatively prohibited discrimination on the basis of HIV status by recipients of state financial assistance,[41] much as the federal Rehabilitation Act prohibits discrimination on the basis of handicap by recipients of federal financial assistance. The significance of this kind of provision is that Medicaid—medical payments on behalf of those who do not have the means to afford to pay for their medical care or to purchase insurance for that purpose—is state money. Thus, a dentist who accepts Medicaid dollars would be bound by the state's nondiscrimination provision because of the receipt of state financial assistance, yet another ground on which to pursue treatment access.

This notion of medical and dental service providers being public accommodations took a dramatic turn with the enactment of the Americans with Disabilities Act. Because that act will so seriously change the way the law has viewed the issues in this and other chapters, a full chapter has been devoted to it later in this book.

NOTES

1. Pub. Law 88-352.

2. *Dimiceli & Sons Funeral Home v. N.Y.C. Commission on Human Rights*, NY Sup. Ct., N.Y. Cty., Index No. 19527/86, January 9, 1987. See *AIDS Update*, Lambda Legal Defense and Education Fund, Inc., No. 15 (February 1987), pp. 3-4.

3. See *AIDS Update*, Lambda Legal Defense and Education Fund, Inc., Vol. 2, No. 1 (June/July 1987), p. 7.

4. *Doe v. Lacarenza Funeral Home*, CT Super. Ct., Jud. Dist. of Stamford/Norwalk at Stamford, Docket No. CV 87 0090916S, filed January 15, 1988. See *AIDS Update*, Lambda Legal Defense and Education Fund, Inc., Vol. 2, No. 6 (March 1988), p. 10.

5. *Doe v. Centinela Hospital et al.*, C.D. Ca., No. 02514 PAR, January 10, 1989. See *AIDS Update*, Lambda Legal Defense and Education Fund, Inc., Vol. 2, No. 1 (June/July 1987), p. 6.

6 *Id.* See *AIDS Update*, Lambda Legal Defense and Education Fund, Inc., Vol. 2, No. 10 (July 1988), p. 8.

7. *Id.* See *AIDS Update*, Lambda Legal Defense and Education Fund, Inc., Vol. 3, No. 5 (February 1989), p. 8.

8. *Luft v. Nail Gallery and All That Glitters*, MD Comm. on Human Relations, No. PA787-C0083-PH-69, September 30, 1988. See *AIDS Update*, Lambda Legal Defense and Education Fund, Inc., Vol. 3, No. 3 (November 1988), p. 7.

9. *Walsh v. Cicmanec*, CA Sup. Ct., San Diego Cty., No. 608500, filed January 31, 1989. See *AIDS Update*, Lambda Legal Defense and Education Fund, Inc., Vol. 3, No. 7 (April/May 1989), p. 1.

10. *White v. Marcus Garvey Nursing Home*, NY Sup. Ct., Kings Cty., Index No. 6600/89, March 20, 1989. See *AIDS Update*,

Lambda Legal Defense and Education Fund, Inc., Vol. 3, No. 7 (April/May 1989), p. 2.

11. *Doe v. A Skilled Nursing Facility*, NY Div. of Human Rights, No. 9K–P–D–89–135752. See *AIDS Lit. Rptr.*, July 13, 1990, p. 4755.

12. *Irving Porter et al. v. David Axelrod, M.D., as Commissioner of the New York State Department of Health, et al.*, NY Sup. Ct., N.Y. Cty., filed November 26, 1990. See *AIDS Lit. Rptr.*, December 28, 1990, p. 5542.

13. "Ban on first-aid calls angers AIDS activists," an Associated Press story appearing in the *Fort Lauderdale Sun-Sentinel*, August 7, 1991, p. 3A.

14. "AIDS calls ban ends," *Fort Lauderdale Sun-Sentinel*, August 22, 1991, p. 3A.

15. *Campanella v. Hurwitz, D.D.S.*, N.Y. City Comm. on Human Rights, Case No. GA–000211030487–DN, decided February 22, 1988. See *AIDS Update*, Lambda Legal Defense and Education Fund, Inc., Vol. 2, No. 6 (March 1988), p. 10.

16. "Dentist's HIV Prejudice Violated New York Law," *The Advocate*, No. 585 (September 10, 1991), p. 17.

17. *Id.*

18. *Whittacre v. The Northern Dispensary*, N.Y. City Comm. on Human Rights, No. AU00015021387, August 17, 1988. See *AIDS Update*, Lambda Legal Defense and Education Fund, Inc., Vol. 3, No. 2 (October 1988), p. 8.

19. *Elstein v. State Division of Human Rights*, NY Sup. Ct., Onondaga Cty., N.Y.L.J., August 18, 1988. See *AIDS Update*, Lambda Legal Defense and Education Fund, Inc., Vol. 3, No. 1 (September 1988), p. 8, and *AIDS Lit. Rptr.*, September 23, 1988, p. 1494.

20. *Id.*, NY Sup. Ct., App. Div., 4th Dept., No. 293. See *AIDS Lit. Rptr.*, June 8, 1990, p. 4607.

21. *In the Matter of G.S. and Baksh*, IL Human Rights Comm., Charge No. 1987CP0113, September 28, 1988. See *AIDS Update*, Lambda Legal Defense and Education Fund, Inc., Vol. 3, No. 3 (November 1988), p. 7.

22. *Sommers v. Breuckheimer*, FL Dept. of Professional Regulation, Case No. 0108948. See *AIDS Lit. Rptr.*, September 28, 1990, p. 5102.

23. *Rosalie Glanz, Executrix of the Estate of Raymond Vadnais v. Vernick et al.*, D. Mass., No. 89–0748–MA. See *AIDS Lit. Rptr.*, December 14, 1990, p. 5481.

24. *Id.* See *AIDS Lit. Rptr.*, February 22, 1991, p. 5845, and *AIDS Update*, Lambda Legal Defense and Education Fund, Inc., Vol. 4, No. 4 (March 1991), p. 4.

25. See *AIDS Lit. Rptr.*, April 26, 1991, p. 6172.

26 *John Doe v. Pleasant Dental Centers*, NJ Super. Ct., Atlantic City, No. ATL–L–002880–91. See *AIDS Lit. Rptr.*, June 28, 1991, p. 6474.

27. *Doe v. Howard County Medical Society*, Howard Cty. (MD) Human Rights Commission, HRC No. 90–001–002, OHR No. 89–02–008. See *AIDS Lit. Rptr.*, October 26, 1990, p. 5248.

28. *The Advocate*, No. 556 (July 13, 1990), p. 18.

29. *Doe v. Kahala Dental Group*, HI Cir. Ct., 1st Cir., No. 89–3436–11. See *AIDS Lit. Rptr.*, December 8, 1989, p. 3751.

30. *Id.* See *AIDS Lit. Rptr.*, August 10, 1990, p. 4905.

31. *Doe v. Kahala Dental Group et al.*, HI Sup. Ct., No. 14647. See *AIDS Lit. Rptr.*, June 24, 1991, p. 6467.

32. *Martell v. North Shore University Hospital*, NY Div. of Human Rights, Case No. 9K–P–ADMS–107810–85. See *AIDS Lit. Rptr.*, September 14, 1990, p. 5028.

33. *Doe v. Washington University et al.*, E.D. Mo., No. 88–2509–C–4, November 30, 1988. See *AIDS Update*, Lambda Legal Defense and Education Fund, Inc., Vol. 3, No. 5 (February 1989), pp. 3–4.

34. "Tuberculosis Cases Soaring," *Fort Lauderdale Sun-Sentinel*, June 24, 1990, p. 6A.

35. "Many Doctors Say They Fear to Treat HIV Patients," an Associated Press story appearing in *The Miami Herald*, June 25, 1990, p. 4A, and "Study: Doctors Avoid HIV Treatment Out of Fear, Prejudice," *The Weekly News*, July 4, 1990, p. 30.

36. "National Panel Calls for 'Dramatic' Expansion of Rural AIDS Programs," *The Weekly News*, August 29, 1990, p. 42.

37. See *AIDS Lit. Rptr.*, September 14, 1990, p. 5032.

38. *Raymond Lyall v. Thomas Balshi, D.D.S.*, PA Human Relations Comm. No. P–3422. See *AIDS Lit. Rptr.*, November 23, 1990, p. 5410.

39. "Policy Statement on AIDS, HIV Infection, and the Practice of Dentistry," American Dental Association, October 12, 1988.

40. See n. 22, *supra*.

41. See, for example, Section 760.50, Florida Statutes (1989).

17

Quarantine

Isolation or quarantine was viewed as a reasonable solution to the control of infectious diseases when such waves of illness as leprosy, tuberculosis, and plague struck. When HIV disease was first identified, it was only natural that those who chose to pay greater heed to fear and ignorance than to medical facts, reason, and civil liberties would turn to such measures. Fortunately, those voices advocating such measures have been fewer than was feared and have been generally unsuccessful.

Quarantine has been more the subject of discussion than implementation. And as one might expect, the usual targets of quarantine efforts have been society's least popular minorities, which all too often are also those with the least political power: prostitutes (of both sexes), promiscuous gay men, and intravenous drug users.

For example, in early 1987, after a Mississippi grand jury declined to indict an HIV-positive male prostitute on felony sodomy charges, health officials issued a quarantine order and forbade the man from having sexual relations without informing his partner of his HIV infection.[1]

At about the same time, a circuit court judge in Florida quarantined an HIV-positive 14-year-old in the psychiatric ward of a state mental hospital because the teenager was allegedly sexually active. After an outcry from AIDS activists, the local ACLU, and others, the judge released the young man.[2]

In mid-1988, a South Carolina woman was quarantined immediately after her release from a mental institution. The quarantine was to her own trailer and for an indefinite period of time, but she left the premises because her electricity was off. She was then quarantined by the state health department.[3] The case was complicated by the woman's consent to voluntary commitment signature after the quarantine order was issued, and the case, thus, offers little in the way of legal precedent. The notion of quarantine to one's own residence, however, as was attempted in the noted South Carolina case, does raise some interesting potential solutions to the possibility of HIV-infected individuals continuing practices that risk further spread of the virus.

Those who argue in favor of quarantine focus on what they call "noncompliants," those who have the virus, who have been counseled, urged, and even ordered to refrain from repeating activity that risks further spread of the virus and who nevertheless, even defiantly, refuse to do so. The examples most often cited are the prostitute who knows that he or she is HIV-positive and who won't stop turning tricks; the promiscuous gay male who knows that he is HIV-positive and who, out of recklessness or viciousness, refuses to stop having unprotected sex; the intravenous drug user who continues to share needles even after being told of an HIV-positive status and of the consequences of further needle sharing.

The answer, however, is not to authorize whole classes of people to have their civil liberties abused by some possibly overzealous or ill-intentioned health department bureaucrat or even by some well-meaning crusader for the stop or spread of disease. Confinement to one's own residence seems to make sense and be a far less restrictive alternative than some other proposals. Some judges have used a technique called "house arrest," with the defendant wearing a wrist or ankle bracelet that emits an electronic signal if he or she leaves the premises other than with permission. Moreover, law enforcement or health officials patrol periodically to ensure that the residence is not itself being used for prostitution or other activities that may risk transmission of the virus.

Officials in Madison County, Illinois, confronted this issue in April 1991 when presented with the situation of an HIV-positive prostitute who persisted in soliciting for unsafe sex even though she knew of her HIV status and the risks of unsafe sex. State health officials had asked for her arrest, and the woman was given her choice of jail or quarantine. She chose the latter and has been quarantined in a state hospital for an indefinite period.[4]

Still, though, some insist on the directions that most jurisdictions have rejected. As late as December 1990, health officials in Salt Lake City, Utah, proposed the quarantine of persons convicted of prostitution who test positive for HIV antibodies. The proposal envisioned all persons convicted of prostitution being required to undergo HIV-antibody testing. Those later convicted of soliciting for sex would then be placed in a "mandatory treatment facility" for "recalcitrant" people.[5] It sounds all too familiar.

NOTES

1. *The New York Times,* February 13, 1987, p. B4.
2. *Pensacola News Journal,* June 12, 1987, p. 1–A.
3. *Doe v. Sercy,* D.S.C., No. 3:88–1068–16, filed May 3, 1988.
4. *The Advocate,* No. 578 (June 4, 1991), p. 26.
5. "Activists Condemn Salt Lake City's HIV Quarantine Plan," *The Advocate,* No. 570 (February 12, 1991), p. 16.

18

Testing

Early in the AIDS chronology, widespread mandatory testing became an easy answer but one that many AIDS authorities considered shortsighted. In that "circle-the-wagons" mentality, testing was the entry point into the testing/labeling/isolation process for those who perceived themselves to be in no danger except from the "perverts and druggies."

The federal government was, unfortunately, one of the prime advocates of this approach. In late 1985, the Department of Defense announced an HIV-antibody testing program for all military recruits and active duty personnel.[1] Little over a year later, the State Department announced plans to begin testing foreign service applicants and current departmental employees and their older dependents—the first such program for civilian federal employees. Applicants who were HIV-positive were to be rejected; current employees who tested HIV-positive and exhibited immune system suppression were not to be assigned overseas; those who were HIV-positive but asymptomatic would be considered on a case-by-case basis.[2]

At about the same time, the Department of Labor announced that students, applicants, and staff working or applying for work with the Job Corps would be tested for HIV antibodies. According to *The New York Times*, the policy stemmed from concerns that the Job Corps centers might become "breeding grounds" for AIDS because many of the students had been IV drug users or had had homosexual encounters.[3]

Challenges have been mounted to the State Department and Job Corps HIV-antibody testing policies. In August 1987, the U.S. Court of Appeals for the District of Columbia Circuit, that court organizationally one rung below and considered by many as closest to the U.S. Supreme Court, upheld the State Department's testing program.[4]

As to the Job Corps, its policy too was challenged.[5] Prior to a ruling, the testing policy was modified in April 1989, seemingly as a result of the early criticism. Nevertheless, the policy still includes testing of all applicants. The modifications adopted extended to excluding only those HIV-positive applicants who pose a risk. One can only guess how that criterion will be defined.

Outside the federal government, testing issues have surfaced in many respects. May 1988 saw three cases of unauthorized testing filed in Pennsylvania. One involved an unauthorized HIV-antibody test of a patient being seen in conjunction with an eye infection and who was exhibiting no HIV symptoms,[6] the second involved an unauthorized HIV-antibody test performed in conjunction with a premarital syphilis test,[7] and the third involved an unauthorized HIV-antibody test in conjunction with treatment for a skin rash.[8] None of the patients received counseling. All sought both compensatory and punitive damages. Among the bases for the suits were invasion of privacy, breach of contract, breach of duty to deal in good faith, negligence, intentional infliction of emotional distress, negligent infliction of emotional distress, and battery.

One of the better known testing cases involved the mandatory testing for HIV antibodies of workers at a Nebraska facility for the retarded. In April 1988, a federal court permanently enjoined that broad-brush approach;[9] the trial court's ruling was upheld by the U.S. Court of Appeals, and the U.S. Supreme Court declined to hear a further appeal of the case in the fall of 1989.[10] The testing program was held to be violative of rights against unreasonable searches, and the Court of Appeals ruling was the first at that federal appellate level to declare unconstitutional a program of HIV-antibody testing.

In a less well-known case in 1988, a state judge in Utah ordered a defendant to take an HIV-antibody test as a condition of sentencing. The defendant had been convicted of disorderly conduct for masturbating in a public park rest room—an activity that hardly risks transmission of the virus. The defendant went into federal court and had the testing order set aside.[11]

Testing has also been the subject of cases because of the treatment of test results. In mid-1988, a Kansas court restrained a health maintenance organization from disclosing an insured's HIV-antibody test results to the insured's estranged wife.[12] This was apparently the first time that a health-care provider had been enjoined as to the release of test results.

Moreover, in mid-1989, an employee filed suit against his Maryland employer after a most egregious set of circumstances. The employer had required the employee to take an HIV-antibody test and further required that the test be performed by the employer's supervisor's own doctor. When the results came back positive for HIV antibodies, the employer was told of those results. The employer then publicized the employee's infected status and reportedly told the employee that he "should go out and shoot himself," adding "I know where you can get a gun."[13]

And state statutory efforts to require testing of classes of individuals have undergone serious legal scrutiny. Illinois enacted legislation to require HIV-antibody testing of persons convicted of certain sex-related crimes. The statute included some crimes that involve absolutely no risk of transmission of HIV, such as running a house of prostitution and fondling a person through clothing. A state court held the testing scheme unconstitutional as a violation of the right to privacy, the right to be free from unreasonable searches and seizures, and the right to equal protection under law.[14] The Illinois Supreme Court has now been petitioned to overturn that ruling.[15]

Notwithstanding the Illinois case, perhaps out of a sincere but misplaced motivation regarding victims' rights or more likely out of motivation to exploit public fears and prejudices, some political figures continue to pursue this kind of testing. The attorney general of Florida even proposed that persons accused of sex-related crimes—not convicted of the crime but just indicted or against whom a criminal information has been filed—be required to be tested for HIV antibodies. Despite all logic that testing the (alleged) perpetrator is the wrong approach and even after having been made aware of the Illinois rejection of a less suspect law, the Florida Legislature enacted the proposal into law in 1990 with only a few modifications.[16]

In 1991, Louisiana joined the ranks of the states that by statute permit testing of persons merely accused of certain crimes.[17] And the District of Columbia Court of Appeals added that jurisdiction to those ranks with a June 1991 ruling.[18]

California's well-known Proposition 96, a part of which allows for mandatory HIV-antibody testing of "persons charged with interfering with the official duties of public safety employees when there is probable cause to believe the person's bodily fluids have mingled with those of the employee," generated an interesting case to test the constitutionality of that provision. In a case involving a deputy sheriff bitten on the arm, a state appellate court upheld that provision, saying that it did not impermissibly violate California's right of privacy.[19]

An even stronger intrusion for the sake of testing occurred in California's *Love* case. That case tested a then-new law requiring HIV-antibody tests for persons convicted of prostitution. It had already been upheld by a trial court and a first-level appellate court when the California Supreme Court issued a stay halting the mandatory tests.[20] The state Supreme Court then remanded the case to the state appellate court, ordering it to reverse its earlier ruling upholding the law.[21] A three-judge panel of that appellate court then nevertheless unanimously affirmed the constitutionality of the statute, saying that it does not violate equal protection rights or constitute an unreasonable search as it meets an "obvious and compelling special need" for public health protection.[22] An appeal was taken again with the California Supreme Court,[23] and the Court rejected that appeal without comment, thus leaving intact the lower appellate court's finding that the statute is constitutional.[24]

Illinois became one of the few states to enact legislation requiring premarital blood tests to include a test for HIV antibodies. After having been in effect for only four months, 4 out of 12,000 applicants had tested HIV-positive, and the number of Illinois marriage license applications was down by 40%.[25] The requirement was dropped in September 1989, and the number of marriage license applications returned to prior levels for the first time as of December 1990.[26]

Testing issues have also generated a few of the more bizarre cases. In June 1987, a medical testing firm reported via telephone to a test subject that the subject had been found positive for HIV antibodies. That was done despite the fact that there was no confirmation of the news recipient's identity over the telephone and no posttest counseling conducted, both allegedly in violation of applicable testing regulations. The test results were a false positive. The test subject sued, with a resulting settlement of $75,000.[27]

And in a case where an HIV-positive man was convicted of exploitation for paying to take Polaroid photographs of a 16-year-old boy and patronizing a juvenile prostitute by offering to pay money, the defendant's treatment included the HIV-antibody test, the results of which were made public.[28] The Washington state Supreme Court reversed the trial court's order for the HIV-antibody test on the basis of the defendant's privacy rights, finding that a 1988 HIV-antibody test would be of no use in corroborating testimony as to sex alleged to have occurred in 1987.[29]

An Alabama law that allows physicians to test for HIV antibodies without the patient's consent is under legal challenge by an AIDS service group in that state. The challenge asserts that the law violates patients' right to approve treatment.[30]

In a personal injury suit in New York, the defendant claimed that HIV infection could impact future expense damages in that the plaintiff was a "prime candidate" for HIV infection. Its motion to have the plaintiff tested for HIV was rejected by the court, which said that the motion was "grounded in speculation and stereotype."[31]

In discussing when judges may order an HIV-antibody test of a criminal defendant, Judge Mary C. Morgan of the Municipal Court of San Francisco says that "[t]here is no basis for testing 'categories' or people such as all gay men, all intravenous drug users, all prostitutes, or all sex offenders. Probable cause must relate to the *individual* under consideration. [Applicable case law] prohibits a search on the mere chance that a person is HIV-positive."[32]

As we examine these legal issues related to testing, it is important to understand why mandatory testing evokes such vehement opposition. The mere prospect of an HIV-antibody test causes great fear in many, even though identifying those in need of treatment and then undertaking the appropriate medical procedures is essential in helping those already infected. And as the *Brogan* case[33] reminds us, test results are usually but not always absolutely accurate. Indeed, a survey of AIDS screening labs by the U.S. Centers for Disease Control showed that most do an accurate job of identifying HIV-infected blood, with the report finding that the labs correctly identified 99.8% of samples that carried the AIDS virus and 99.4% that were free of HIV.[34]

As we have seen, discrimination against those who have AIDS, ARC, or even just asymptomatic HIV infection is widespread. The consequences of knowledge of one's infection can be loss of employment (and loss of dignity that is attendant to being a part of the work force), loss in income, uninsurability, unavailability of professional—including medical and dental—services, and so on. Instead of extending a special helping hand to those infected with HIV, too much of society still shuns them.

And the news of HIV-positive status is still seen by too many as an automatic death sentence. News of medical progress is slow to reach those unwilling to hear it, and many remain unaware of very successful treatments of HIV-positive persons who obtain medical treatment before symptoms occur. Indeed, there are reports that show the suicide rate has tripled among those who are told that they are HIV-positive.

With that background in mind, it should come as no surprise that anything but anonymous, voluntary HIV-antibody testing effectively drives underground those most in need of testing. Several studies have borne out this conclusion.[35] Those most likely to have already been infected and who are therefore now in need of medical attention before their symptoms become unmanageable are afraid to become involved in the HIV identification and treatment process because they want to continue to work, to be insured, to live their lives as usual.

We have had only a few years of history on this issue. But we already know that AIDS/HIV education at every level and the availability of low-cost or free, anonymous HIV-antibody testing, coupled with mandatory pretest and posttest counseling, remain the manner in which those most in need of testing and possible treatment will be most likely to pursue these important steps.

Still, despite all of the progress that has been made toward understanding these issues, as recently as mid-1990, the Arizona Medical Association called for mandatory HIV-antibody testing for gays and prostitutes, even though the state health department said it opposes implementation of the resolution.[36] And in what appears to be a better reasoned, less discriminatory approach, an editorial in the May 1991 issue of the *New England Journal of Medicine* recommended routine AIDS screening of all hospital patients, health-care workers, pregnant women, and newborns.[37] Some of these issues are explained more fully in Chapter 22, "The Right to Know."

NOTES

1. "Memorandum: Military Implementation of Public Health Service Provisional Recommendations Concerning Testing Blood and Plasma for Antibodies to HTLV-III," March 13, 1985.

2. See *AIDS Update*, Lambda Legal Defense and Education Fund, Inc., No. 13 (December 1986), pp. 7–8.

3. *Ibid.*, p. 8.

4. *Local 1812, AFGE, v. Department of State*, 662 F.Supp. 50 (D.D.C. 1987).

5. *Dorsey v. U.S. Dept. of Labor et al.*, D.D.C., filed July 12, 1988.

6. *Doe v. Wills Eye Hospital and Wieland*, PA Ct. of Common Pleas, Philadelphia Cty., No. 5248, filed March 30, 1988. See *AIDS Update*, Lambda Legal Defense and Education Fund, Inc., Vol. 2, No. 8 (May 1988), p. 4.

7. *Doe v. Dyer-Goode*, PA Ct. of Common Pleas, Philadelphia Cty., No. 529, filed March 30, 1988. See *AIDS Update*, Lambda Legal Defense and Education Fund, Inc., Vol. 2, No. 8 (May 1988), p. 4.

8. *Doe v. Conly and Geisinger Clinic*, M.D. Pa., CV–88–0486, filed March 31, 1988. See *AIDS Update*, Lambda Legal Defense and Education Fund, Inc., Vol. 2, No. 8 (May 1988), p. 4.

9. *Glover et al. v. Eastern Nebraska Community Office of Retardation (ENCOR)*, 867 F.2d 461 (8th Cir. 1989).

10. *Eastern Nebraska Community Office of Retardation v. Glover*, cert. denied 58 U.S.L.W. 3287 (October 30, 1989).

11. *Barrows v. Van Sciver*, UT Cir. Ct., 3rd Jud. Dist., Salt Lake City, filed August 30, 1988.

12. *Doe v. Prime Health Kansas City, Inc.*, KS Dist. Ct., Johnson Cty., No. 88 C5149, May 17, 1988. See *AIDS Update*, Lambda Legal Defense and Education Fund, Inc., Vol. 2, No. 9, p. 8.

13. *Buler v. Southland Corp.*, MD Cir. Ct., Baltimore City. See *AIDS Update*, Lambda Legal Defense and Education Fund, Inc., Vol. 3, No. 9 (July 1989), pp. 2–3.

14. *People v. Madison and Adams*, IL Cir. Ct., Cook Cty., 1st Mun. Div., Nos. 88–123613 and 87–2281577, August 3, 1989. See *AIDS Update*, Lambda Legal Defense and Education Fund, Inc., Vol. 3, No. 10 (August 1989), p. 7, and *AIDS Lit. Rptr.*, August 11, 1989, pp. 3, 122.

15. *Illinois v. Adams and Madison*, IL Sup. Ct., No. 69278. See *AIDS Lit. Rptr.*, February 8, 1991, p. 5782.

16. Chapter 90–210, Laws of Florida.

17. *The Advocate*, No. 582 (July 30, 1991), p. 29.

18. *The Advocate*, No. 582 (July 30, 1991), p. 28.

19. *Johnetta J. v. Municipal Court*, CA Ct. of App., No. 1137078. See *AIDS Update*, Lambda Legal Defense and Education Fund, Inc., Vol. 4, No. 2 (July 1990), p. 1.

20. *Love et al. v. Superior Court of the City and County of San Francisco*, CA Sup. Ct., No. 609, 1/4 A050880, S017387. See *AIDS Lit. Rptr.*, September 28, 1990, p. 5096.

21. See *AIDS Lit. Rptr.*, November 9, 1990, p. 5331.

22. See *AIDS Lit. Rptr.*, January 11, 1991, p. 5614.

23. *Love et al., v. Superior Court of the City and County of San Francisco*, CA Sup. Ct., No. S017387. See *AIDS Lit. Rptr.*, February 22, 1991, p. 5848.

24. *Ibid.*, See *AIDS Lit. Rptr.*, March 22, 1991, p. 6001.

25. See *AIDS Update*, Lambda Legal Defense and Education Fund, Inc., Vol. 2, No. 8 (May 1988), pp. 3–4.

26. *The Advocate*, No. 570 (February 12, 1991), p. 25.

27. *Brogan v. Kimberly Services, Inc. et al.*, CA Super. Ct., San Francisco Cty., No. 893414. See *AIDS Lit. Rptr.*, January 11, 1991, p. 5627.

28. "Appeals Court Upholds 'Extremely Harsh' Jail Term for Gay PWA," *The Weekly News*, March 20, 1991, p. 15.

29. *State of Washington v. Farmer*, WA Sup. Ct., No. 56583-0, *en banc*. See *AIDS Lit. Rptr.*, March 8, 1991, p. 5917.

30. *The Advocate*, No. 581 (July 16, 1991), p. 32.

31. *Subran v. J&S Management Inc.*, NY Sup. Ct., Kings Cty., IA Part 8. See *AIDS Lit. Rptr.*, July 26, 1991, p. 6591.

32. Morgan, Judge Mary C., "The Problems of Testing for HIV in the Criminal Courts," *Judges' Journal*, Vol. 29, No. 2 (Spring 1990), p. 25.

33. See n. 27, *supra*.

34. "Tuberculosis Cases Soaring," *Fort Lauderdale Sun-Sentinel*, June 24, 1990, p. 6A.

35. See *e.g.*, "The Impact of Mandatory Reporting of HIV Seropositive Persons in South Carolina," a paper presented at the IV International Conference on AIDS, June 12–16, 1988, Stockholm, Sweden; and "Mandatory Reporting of HIV Testing Would Deter Men from Being Tested," *Journal of the American Medical Association*, Vol. 261, No. 9 (March 3, 1989), pp. 1275–1276.

36. *The Advocate*, No. 556 (July 31, 1990), p. 17.

37. "Widespread Testing for AIDS Suggested," an Associated Press story appearing in *The Miami Herald*, May 23, 1991, p. 33A.

19

Torts

Torts represents a major area of the law, but one that many nonattorneys would not recognize by that name. A tort is basically a private or civil wrong independent of a contract.[1] It is private or civil in that there is no crime on the basis of which the government may prosecute. Its independence from a contract means that there is no formal agreement governing the parties' rights and obligations. There is instead a relationship that involves one party having a duty to the other and an alleged breach of that duty, with the duty usually arising by operation of law rather than by agreement of the parties.

Probably the most easily recognized example of a tort is a simple automobile accident. Laws and regulations set the standards for driving so that all may safely operate their motor vehicles or proceed as pedestrians. When one car follows another unsafely and rear-ends the car in front or when one wrongly proceeds through a red light and strikes another vehicle or a pedestrian, that is a tort, for which a suit for damages may arise. (Note that there may also be a crime in some cases, such as the example of the car running the red light, but any such crime is a different legal action from the tort.)

Torts are generally divided into several kinds: those that involve some degree of intention to commit them, those that result from negligence rather than intent, and those that result from a product being defective. Examples of intentional torts would be battery, false imprisonment, infliction of emotional distress, and trespass. Torts usually involving a lesser degree of intent but nevertheless some measure of it would be defamation, invasion of privacy, and fraud. And then there is the broad category of torts that result from one party's negligence, such as automobile accidents. A products liability tort could arise because of a product that, when used in the manner in which it is designed to be used, causes injury to the user. There are other kinds of torts, but our objective here is to keep the focus on HIV-related legal issues, and this brief explanation will suffice for that purpose.

Let us look first at those HIV-related torts that involve some measure of intent. Probably the best example involved one man's harassment of an HIV-infected neighbor. He had engaged in verbal harassment for some three years and had encouraged his son to purposely bounce a ball against the window of the plaintiff's home. The HIV-infected plaintiff obtained a restraining order against the harassing neighbor. When the neighbor persisted in the offending conduct, the court fined him $2,000 for violation of that restraining order.[2]

Suit for both intentional and negligent infliction of emotional distress was filed by a Florida man who allegedly contracted HIV disease from his former lover. The suit charged that the plaintiff was faithful during their five-year relationship that he believed was monogamous and that the lover claimed to be free from any transmissible disease even though the lover knew of being HIV-infected for some months without telling the plaintiff. He sued for $20,000 in damages.[3]

There have been several defamation actions on HIV-related issues. In one case, a defendant allegedly told as many as 15 people that the plaintiff had AIDS. One of those others related the report to still others, including the plaintiff's mother. The report spread, eventually generating the plaintiff's avoidance of friends and family, departure from his job, and departure from the small town. He was awarded more than $25,000 in a slander suit, with appeal of the award having been rejected by the Nebraska Supreme Court.[4]

Another defamation suit was filed by a Georgia woman whose photograph with her baby appeared in a 1989 newspaper story about a hospital social worker, the story implying that the woman and her baby had AIDS.[5] The case was settled, with the terms of the settlement not released.[6]

In the only case to date in which the employment of an HIV-positive employee, in this case a physician, has been held to have been properly restricted, a New Jersey court found the physician's estate entitled to money damages from the hospital that breached his rights as a patient. The hospital failed to provide the patient's medical records with the appropriate degree of confidentiality and allowed news of his diagnosis to be spread among his colleagues and the larger community.[7]

Before getting into the long list of cases having to do with allegations about negligence and products liability as to blood and body-fluid substances used to treat hemophiliacs, let us look at one products liability case that dealt with medical equipment and several cases that deal with other kinds of negligence.

The products liability case involved a paramedic who suffered a needle stick while disposing of another needle into a hypodermic-needle disposal box. Claiming that the needle stick resulted from the disposal box being deficiently designed, he alleged possible HIV transmission based on the presence of patients known to have AIDS having been on the floor of the hospital at the time of the incident. However, because he could not show that the specific needle that had jabbed him was one that had actually been used by someone with HIV disease, the judge dismissed the case. Although the plaintiff had tested HIV-negative five times since the needle stick, he alleged that he has lived in constant fear since the incident and that his emotional distress has led to loss of sexual function and deterioration of his marriage.[8]

As we move into the area of negligence, it is interesting to contrast the dismissed needle-stick case with another involving an AIDS patient who bit a security guard during an emergency room scuffle in 1988. As with the needle-stick case, the plaintiff had repeatedly tested HIV-negative. But here, there was no question as to whether the source could have HIV disease. In a suit against the hospital, the court awarded the guard $1.9 million.[9] The West Virginia Supreme Court has agreed to review the decision.[10]

A different kind of needle-stick negligence case arose when a guest at the Baltimore Hyatt Regency pulled down the bed sheet and was allegedly stuck in the leg by a dirty hypodermic needle that "flew" off his bed. He sued the hotel and its parent corporation for $4 million out of fear of contraction of HIV disease.[11] Hyatt denied allegations that it failed to properly provide for the guest's safety and assure prompt medical treatment.[12] The injured guest who sued, himself an attorney, settled the claim for $120,000.[13]

A different kind of negligence resulted in an award for pain and suffering to a hospital worker bitten by a violent state corrections department inmate. The court found that the state had inadequately supervised the inmate. It denied damages, however, on the basis of emotional distress over the possibility that the hospital worker may acquire AIDS as a result of the bite.[14]

Another direction for these HIV-related negligence claims occurred when a California police officer watching an autopsy was splashed in the eye with blood from an HIV-infected corpse. The negligence alleged was on the part of the county medical examiner's office in not providing the observing police officer with a protective mask or garment during the procedure. The officer was awarded $250,000 by the jury for emotional distress, and his wife was awarded an additional $67,000.[15]

Yet another negligence case was brought by a registered nurse who was given an erroneous positive HIV-antibody test result over the telephone. The nurse had taken only the basic ELISA test, which many jurisdictions require to be confirmed before a positive result may be released to the person tested. Moreover, providing the news of the positive result over the telephone without seeking proof of the recipient's identity or providing counseling were alleged as violations of the testing regulations established by the San Francisco Department of Health. The nurse learned that the test results were incorrect only after taking his wife and child to the same testing center for tests of their own.[16] After the court denied any entitlement to punitive damages,[17] the case was settled for $75,000.[18]

Somewhat similarly, a California man was awarded more than $200,000 in a suit alleging that he was falsely diagnosed with ARC and, as a result, suffered severe depression and emotional distress thinking that he was near death.[19]

And a woman who says she was told that she was given a Pap test with a cotton swab previously used on a patient who may have had AIDS sued an Illinois hospital for negligence.[20] There were no indications that she had contracted the virus by the time that she filed her suit.[21] However, the state health department issued two citations against the hospital, and the hospital disciplined a third doctor involved in the case.[22]

Next, we move into a large number of cases involving allegations of negligent transmission of HIV through tainted blood. The law looks at the "duty to others" factor in negligence cases by ascertaining what the standard of care is and then seeing whether that standard was breached in a manner that caused the damages that are the subject of the injured party's claims. Much seems to turn—appropriately—on the issue of when during the AIDS chronology the blood transfusion occurred, with the turning point in these cases seeming to occur in 1983 and 1984.

A federal court directed a verdict in favor of the blood bank and other defendants in a suit for negligence and medical malpractice by a plaintiff who alleged that he was infected by AIDS-tainted blood during surgery in November 1981.[23] That effective dismissal of the case was upheld on appeal as the possibility that AIDS was blood-transmitted was not discovered until some eight months after the plaintiff's operation and was not fully accepted by the medical community until 1984.[24]

Somewhat similarly, the defendant hospital was victorious in a $1.5 million medical malpractice suit brought by a woman who claimed that professional negligence caused her to become infected with HIV during a 1982 blood transfusion. She said the transfusion was performed without her consent; the defense was that there was no system available to screen for HIV prior to 1985.[25]

Noting the trial court's record that when the transfusion had occurred, no blood bank in the country had implemented donor screening methods to eliminate those at high risk for AIDS, a California appellate court in 1991 affirmed a trial court jury's finding that a defendant blood bank had observed all professionally accepted standards when processing blood transfused into an infant after his premature birth in October 1982.[26]

A California jury found that the defendant hospital had followed the standard of care set by blood banks and processors nationwide in 1983 and rejected negligence claims by survivors of a recipient of HIV-tainted blood in that year.[27] Another California jury also found in favor of a defendant blood bank in a suit by a woman who claimed that its screening measures in 1983 were negligent.[28]

A Michigan trial court dismissed a suit by a late 1983 recipient of HIV-tainted blood, saying that the defendant Red Cross and hospital had met all practical standards of care in use at that time and had no reason to know that a transfused unit of blood was infected with HIV.[29]

But a Texas court awarded $121,030 to the mother of a child who died of AIDS in 1985 as a result of having been transfused with HIV-tainted blood shortly after birth in 1983. This different result for a 1983 transfusion was apparently based on the defendant hospital's failure to properly eliminate intravenous drug users from donating blood.[30]

And another Texas jury awarded $800,000 to the HIV-infected widow of a man who died from AIDS contracted through a 1983 blood transfusion administered during a heart operation, finding the hospital's screening methods negligent.[31]

Transfusions that occurred in 1984 also generated mixed results. A January 1984 transfusion of nine units of blood during surgery apparently was the cause of HIV infection of the husband of a widow who sued after she contracted the virus from him. The jury found for the defendant hospital.[32]

But an Ohio court denied a motion by the defendant Red Cross to find in its favor in a suit against it and a local blood service for alleged failure to follow procedures available to screen blood in 1984. The court found that questions of fact remained and ordered the suit to proceed.[33]

Similarly, a New York state court denied a defendant hospital's motion to dismiss a suit arising out of HIV infection through blood transfusion even though tests had not yet been developed to screen blood for HIV at the time of the January 1984 transfusion. The judge indicated that the plaintiff was at least entitled to discover what screening procedures and safeguards, if any, were in place at the blood bank at the time of the transfusion.[34]

The "standard of care" issue came more clearly into play in the case of a 24-year-old woman infected with HIV as a result of a May 1984 transfusion with tainted blood. She alleged that the defendant blood service could have reduced the possibility of her receiving tainted blood via surrogate testing—that is, testing for blood-related viruses closely related to HIV even though no HIV-specific test was then available.[35] The case was settled privately with the terms of the settlement not disclosed.[36]

The standard of care is at issue in another case involving a May 1984 transfusion. In that case, a blood bank, hospital, and attending physicians are alleged to have negligently supplied a child with HIV-tainted blood during a surgical procedure. The standard of care breach alleged by the plaintiffs is that San Francisco-Oakland area blood banks and hospitals failed to live up to a special duty to warn of the high risks involved in transfusions because of the greater than average proportion of high-risk donors in that geographic area.[37]

In a most complex consolidated set of more than 20 liability suits based on allegations of transfusions of HIV-tainted blood, a California trial court judge ruled that the defendant blood bank had a duty to use "reasonable diligence and its best judgment in exercise of its professional skill and the application of its learning." The court imposed a "professional standard of care" and not the standard for ordinary negligence. The blood bank "shall be held to have that degree of learning and skill ordinarily possessed by reputable blood banks practicing in the same or similar locality and under similar circumstances," the court said.[38]

The court found that the plaintiffs had failed to show that the defendant hospital had violated the proper standard of care in a California case based on 1981 transfusions. The hospital had conducted a comprehensive computer-based search to locate blood-transfusion recipients to notify them of the possibility that the blood received may have been HIV-tainted. Moreover, the specific plaintiffs in this case were notified both by telephone and in writing. The court dismissed the case.[39]

An interesting twist to these standard of care cases based on early blood transfusions occurred in a Washington case. It was the first case in which the implicated blood donor testified in court, the case having been brought by a woman who received the HIV-tainted blood after giving birth in August 1984. The blood donor was a gay medical professional who was in what he thought was a monogamous 22-year relationship. Identifying himself as a committed blood donor who had given more than 20 times before being diagnosed as HIV-positive, he testified that he would not have donated in 1984 if the blood center had asked all gay men, or all who could not guarantee that their relationship was monogamous, to refrain from donating blood. The plaintiff was awarded $1.8 million by the jury.[40]

Still focusing on the standard of care, a jury awarded $12 million to a plaintiff who received HIV-tainted blood during surgery to correct a back ailment in March 1985. The blood had been collected by the Red Cross on the same day that the agency received HIV-antibody testing kits. Moreover, the plaintiff had made an apparently unused autologous blood donation—a donation of her own blood to be used in case she needed a transfusion—and there was expert testimony that the transfusion was simply unnecessary.[41] The Ohio Court of Appeals affirmed the award.[42]

As is demonstrated in the last case, there is a much stronger likelihood of an award to a plaintiff recipient of HIV-infected blood if some factor involving what may legally be or what appears even in a lay sense to be medical malpractice is involved over and above any negligence in furnishing or administering HIV-tainted blood. For example, in a case where the wife/mother and 13-month-old son had already died and the husband/father was HIV-positive, a federal court ruled that the negligent failure of a Navy hospital to monitor a fetus and perform a caesarean delivery in time was a direct cause of factors contributing to the mother's excessive blood loss, which led to the tainted transfusions in 1981. Even though HIV was not a known risk factor then, the underlying negligence generated the liability for the HIV infection of the wife/mother and ultimately the other family members.[43] The court awarded the Naval officer $2.7 million.[44]

In another suit against the Navy, it was negligence during a 1983 tonsillectomy on a 12-year-old boy that caused the need for a significant increase in the number of units of blood required to be infused. Some of those units were HIV-tainted, and the boy and his family were awarded more than $1 million.[45]

Similarly, a jury awarded $970,000 to a 29-year-old man infected with HIV from tainted blood obtained through a blood service that accepted the tainted blood after having rejected blood from the same donor on three prior occasions and having done so for reasons that should have disqualified him from making any blood donations.[46] The jury award was reduced by the court to $437,293 total, including fees.[47]

An Arizona jury made what was then apparently the largest award—$28.7 million—for negligent infection to a 5-year-old and the child's parents in which the child acquired HIV through tainted red blood cells improperly diluted with HIV-tainted plasma and where the transfusion was per-

formed without parental consent. On a prior occasion when
the child had needed a transfusion, the parents had offered
their own blood.[48] The jury award was reduced by $1.8 mil-
lion to $26.9 million by the judge,[49] and the parties ulti-
mately settled for $6 million, with no admission of wrongdo-
ing, to avoid lengthy appeals.[50]

Likewise, a California jury awarded more than $3 million
to a ten-year-old infected with HIV-tainted blood during
open-heart surgery in 1984 in a suit alleging negligence in
the failure to advise the child's family of the available direct
donor program, the failure to delay the procedure until the
then-new HIV-antibody test could be done, and the failure
to advise of the risks and hazards of blood transfusions.[51]

Yet another example of the interplay of medical malpractice and HIV-tainted blood occurred when a mix-up of two
patients with the same last name caused the wrong man to
receive the HIV-infected blood of the other.[52]

And an Illinois jury awarded $2.4 million to a 52-year-old
man and his wife in a case in which the husband was treated
in 1984 for a condition unrelated to AIDS but in which the
physician negligently prescribed a drug that caused pancrea-
titis ultimately requiring blood transfusions that were the
source of the man's HIV infection.[53]

An unusual mode of further transmission came into play
in a Pennsylvania case filed against the Red Cross, a local
hospital, and others over an alleged transmission well after
medical experts knew about HIV. The case involved the
transfusion of apparently HIV-tainted blood to a wife/
mother in 1988 and her subsequent passage of HIV to one
child through breast-feeding and to another who was con-
ceived before the mother discovered her own HIV infection.
There are allegations that the transfusions were medially unnecessary, were executed without the recipient's informed
consent, and that the hospital gave what the plaintiff wife/
mother asserts was an express warranty that the blood was
not contaminated with HIV.[54]

But the hospital was dismissed as a defendant and therefore could not be found liable for damages in a suit brought
by a blood center and the estate of a deceased recipient of

HIV-tainted blood in which the hospital relied on a defendant that was also a blood bank and that had notified the hospital that it, the second blood bank, was following federal regulations and guidelines.[55]

Next, let's move on from blood as the transmitting agent to one called "Factor VIII." Factor VIII is the substance administered to hemophiliacs to alleviate their blood-clotting problems. And the history on the Factor VIII cases reflects the same reactions to standards of care and the time of the alleged transmissions as did the blood cases.

In a suit against a pharmaceutical company for damages for its failure to warn the public in December 1982 of AIDS-related risks associated with its Factor VIII products, a federal court jury found in favor of the defendant pharmaceutical company.[56] But a motion for a new trial has been granted in that case.[57]

An Alaska jury returned a verdict for the defense in a suit by a hemophiliac who claimed that the defendant pharmaceutical firm failed to warn him of dangers associated with its Factor VIII product in 1982 and 1983.[58]

Still awaiting resolution as of this writing is a case brought in Georgia against the same pharmaceutical company. This case was brought by a hemophiliac who used the defendant's product exclusively through a program operated by a local hemophilia agency for a period of at least six years prior to 1986 and who subsequently tested HIV-positive.[59]

And the negligence involved in these tort cases may also be an omission instead of an overt act. For example, a couple sued a hospital, the Red Cross, and a doctor who operated on the husband in 1984. Although the doctor was told in 1987 that the husband had received HIV-tainted plasma during the procedure, the information was never passed along to the husband/patient.[60]

The newest direction for tort litigation involving HIV disease focuses on health-care workers who kept practicing their professions even though they knew, suspected, or perhaps should have known that they were HIV-positive. A detailed discussion of some of the issues related to these tort cases can be found in Chapter 22 of this volume, with the well-known case brought by Kimberly Bergalis discussed in that chapter.

One of the first of the other such cases to be decided was a class action suit brought by former patients of a Delaware dentist who died of AIDS. The defense moved to have the case dismissed, while the class of former patients sought an injunction to freeze the dentist's estate to help pay for testing and treatment that the multiple plaintiffs might require.[61]

In another case, a Maryland court dismissed multiple suits against the estate of a surgeon in which the suits claimed that the plaintiffs were negligently exposed to HIV when the surgeon operated on them even though he knew he was HIV-positive. The court cited a Pennsylvania decision holding that potential exposure to HIV was not a compensable injury, especially when the plaintiffs failed to show signs of infection more than six months after their potential exposure.[62]

And a class action suit has been filed against two Pennsylvania hospitals and the subject physician charging negligence for possible exposure to patients, spouses, and children by an obstetrics-gynecological resident who tested positive for HIV antibodies.[63]

NOTES

1. *Black's Law Dictionary*, 4th Ed., West Publishing Company, 1951.

2. *Henly v. Kiss*, CA Super. Ct., San Francisco Cty., No. 915924. See *AIDS Lit. Rptr.*, October 26, 1990, p. 5253.

3. *Hill v. Miller*, FL Cir. Ct., Orange Cty., No. CI–90–5455 #32. See *AIDS Lit. Rptr.*, August 24, 1990, p. 4958.

4. *McCune v. Neitzel*, NE Sup. Ct., No. 88–552. See *AIDS Lit. Rptr.*, August 10, 1990, p. 4904.

5. *Hammonds v. Cox Enterprises, Inc., d/b/a The Atlanta Journal*, GA Super. Ct., Fulton Cty., No. D80918. See *AIDS Lit. Rptr.*, September 14, 1990, p. 5031.

6. *Id.* See *AIDS Lit. Rptr.*, March 22, 1991, p. 6005.

7. *Estate of William Behringer v. The Medical Center at Prin-*

ceton et al., NJ Super. Ct., Law Div., Mercer Cty., No. L88–2550. See *AIDS Lit. Rptr.*, May 10, 1991, p. 6245.

8. *Burk v. Sage Products, Inc.*, E.D. Pa., No. 90–3077. See *AIDS Lit. Rptr.*, December 14, 1990, p. 5487.

9. *Johnson v. West Virginia University Hospitals, Inc.*, WVA Cir. Ct., Monongalia Cty., No. CA–89–C–109. See *AIDS Lit. Rptr.*, January 12, 1990, p. 3844.

10. *Id.*, WVA Sup. Ct., No. 19678. See *AIDS Lit. Rptr.*, July 13, 1990, p. 4749.

11. *Doe v. Hyatt Hotels Corp. et al.*, D. Md., No. MJG–90–1071. See *AIDS Lit. Rptr.*, May 11, 1990, p. 4465.

12. *Id.* See *AIDS Lit. Rptr.*, June 22, 1990, p. 4696.

13. "Guest at Hyatt to Get $120,000 for Needle Scare," *Baltimore Sun*, May 14, 1991, p. 1D. Subsequently reported as *Bressler v. Hyatt Hotels Corp.* See *AIDS Lit. Rptr.*, June 14, 1991, p. 6394.

14. *Hare v. State of New York*, NY Sup. Ct., App. Div. 3rd Dept., No. 2276E. See *AIDS Lit. Rptr.*, June 28, 1991, p. 6471.

15. *Pavek v. County of Los Angeles*, CA Super. Ct., Los Angeles Cty., Central Div., No. C–675861. See *AIDS Lit. Rptr.*, August 24, 1990, p. 4951.

16. *Brogan v. Kimberly Services, Inc. et al.*, CA Super. Ct., San Francisco Cty., No. 893414. See *AIDS Lit. Rptr.*, September 23, 1988, p. 1500.

17. *Id.* See *AIDS Lit. Rptr.*, August 24, 1990, p. 4955.

18. *Id.* See *AIDS Lit. Rptr.*, January 11, 1991, p. 5627.

19. *Welenken v. SmithKline Bio-Science Laboratories Ltd.*, CA Super. Ct., San Francisco Cty., No. 881107. See *AIDS Lit. Rptr.*, July 12, 1991, p. 6518.

20. *Jane Doe v. Illinois Masonic Hospital*, IL Cir. Ct., Cook Cty., No. 91 L 06294. See *AIDS Lit. Rptr.*, June 14, 1991, p. 6398.

21. *The Miami Herald*, April 25, 1991, p. 16A.

22. "Illinois Warns Hospital," *Fort Lauderdale Sun-Sentinel*, May 9, 1991, p. 3A.

23. *Hoemke v. New York Blood Center et al.*, S.D.N.Y., No. 88 Civ. 9029. See *AIDS Lit. Rptr.*, December 8, 1989, p. 3684.

24. *Id.*, 2nd Cir., No. 90–7182. See *AIDS Lit. Rptr.*, September 14, 1990, p. 5021, and *AIDS Update*, Lambda Legal Defense and Education Fund, Inc., Vol. 4, No. 2 (December 1990), p. 8.

25. *Traxler v. Varady*, CA Super. Ct., Solano Cty., No. 897–257. See *AIDS Lit. Rptr.*, February 22, 1991, p. 5843.

26. *O'Rourke et al. v. Irwin Memorial Blood Bank et al.*, CA

Ct. of App., Dist. 1, Div. 4, No. A047081. See *AIDS Lit. Rptr.*, June 14, 1991, p. 6387.

27. *Murphy et al. v. Community Hospital of the Monterey Peninsula*, CA Super. Ct., Monterey Cty., No. 88715. See *AIDS Lit. Rptr.*, October 12, 1990, p. 5160.

28. *Wilson v. Irwin Memorial Blood Bank*, CA Super. Ct., San Francisco Cty., No. 864-989. See *AIDS Lit. Rptr.*, June 24, 1991, p. 6466.

29. *Anonymous Blood Recipient v. William Beaumont Hospital, Southeastern Michigan Chapter American Red Cross*, MI Cir. Ct., Oakland Cty., No. 89-363705-NH. See *AIDS Lit. Rptr.*, March 8, 1991, p. 5920.

30. *Jackson v. Tarrant Hospital District*, TX Dist. Ct., 48th Jud. Dist., No. 48-95022-86. See *AIDS Lit. Rptr.*, August 10, 1990, p. 4900.

31. *Esther Beeson, individually and as representative of the estate of Thomas W. Beeson v. J.K. and Susie L. Wadley Research Institutes and Blood Bank, d/b/a/ The Blood Center at Wadley, and St. Paul Medical Center*, TX Dist. Ct., 101st Jud. Dist., Dallas Cty., No. 89-04827-E. See *AIDS Lit. Rptr.*, June 28, 1991, p. 6460.

32. *William and Dorothy Polikoff v. Regents of the University of California and UCSD Medical Center*, CA Super. Ct., San Diego Cty., No. 590154. See *AIDS Lit. Rptr.*, December 14, 1990, p. 5482.

33. *Zaccone v. American Red Cross, Northern Ohio Red Cross Blood Services, et al.*, OH Ct. of Common Pleas, Cuyahoga Cty., No. 159169. See *AIDS Lit. Rptr.*, January 11, 1991, p. 5621.

34. *Doe v. University Hospital of the New York University Medical Center et al.*, NY Sup. Ct., N.Y. Cty., IA Part 26. See *AIDS Lit. Rptr.*, August 24, 1990, p. 4953.

35. *Crawford v. United Blood Services of Ventura County et al.*, CA Super. Ct., Ventura Cty., No. 98164. See *AIDS Lit. Rptr.*, August 11, 1989, p. 3123.

36. *Id.* See *AIDS Lit. Rptr.*, February 22, 1991, p. 5845.

37. *Jane Doe et al. v. Blood Bank of Alameda-Contra Costa Medical Association et al.*, CA Super. Ct., Alameda Cty., No. 682090-5. See *AIDS Lit. Rptr.*, July 12, 1991, p. 6524.

38. *Complex Blood Bank Litigation*, CA Super. Ct., San Francisco Cty., No. 908-843. See *AIDS Lit. Rptr.*, July 13, 1990, p. 4744.

39. *Frank Sisseck et al. v. St. Francis Memorial Hospital et al.*, CA Super. Ct., San Francisco, Cty., No. 905361. See *AIDS Lit. Rptr.*, January 25, 1991, p. 5695.

40. *Doe v. Puget Sound Blood Center*, WA Super. Ct., King Cty.,

No. 88–2–10861–7. See *AIDS Lit. Rptr.*, November 9, 1990, p. 5328. Motion for new trial denied. See *AIDS Lit. Rptr.*, January 11, 1991, p. 5619.

41. *Jeanne et al. v. Hawkes Hospital of Mt. Carmel et al.*, OH Common Pleas Ct., Franklin Cty., No. 87–CV–03–1669. See ABA Journal, June 1990, p. 26, and *AIDS Lit. Rptr.*, March 23, 1990, p. 4205. A defense motion to rehear the case was rejected. See *AIDS Lit. Rptr.*, May 11, 1990, p. 4458.

42. OH Ct. of App., 10th Dist., No. 90AP-599. See *AIDS Lit. Rptr.*, June 28, 1991, p. 6459.

43. *Gaffney et al. v. United States*, D. Mass., No. 88–1457–Z. See *AIDS Lit. Rptr.*, May 11, 1990, p. 4457.

44. *Id.* See *AIDS Lit. Rptr.*, April 26, 1991, p. 6162.

45. *Doe et al. v. United States*, D.R.I., No. 86–0179–T. See *AIDS Lit. Rptr.*, May 25, 1990, p. 4540.

46. *Clark v. United Blood Services*, NV Dist. Ct., 2nd Jud. Dist., No. CV–88–6981. See *AIDS Lit. Rptr.*, May 25, 1990, p. 4542.

47. *Id.* See *AIDS Lit. Rptr.*, September 28, 1990, p. 5098.

48. *Edwards et al. v. Samaritan Health Service et al.*, AZ Super. Ct., Maricopa Cty., No. CV–87–35695. See *AIDS Lit. Rptr.*, June 8, 1990, p. 4601.

49. *Edwards et al. v. Kuruvilla et al.* See *AIDS Lit. Rptr.*, June 22, 1990, p. 4686.

50. *Id.* See *AIDS Lit. Rptr.*, August 24, 1990, p. 4951.

51. *Richard Katz, Esq., Guardian Ad Litem of T.E., a minor v. Childrens Hospital of Los Angeles et al.*, CA Super. Ct., Los Angeles Cty., Central Dist., Dept. 20, No. C 683 049. See *AIDS Lit. Rptr.*, September 14, 1990, p. 5024.

52. "AIDS Mistake Costly," *Fort Lauderdale Sun-Sentinel*, June 30, 1990, p. 3A.

53. *Doe v. Massaysay*, IL Cir. Ct., Cook Cty., No. 85 L 13319. See *AIDS Lit. Rptr.*, July 13, 1990, p. 4742.

54. *Stephen and Kathleen Roberts et al. v. American Red Cross et al.*, E.D. Pa., No. 90–6737. See *AIDS Lit. Rptr.*, December 14, 1990, p. 5489.

55. *Krygier v. Airweld Inc.*, NY Sup. Ct., Kings Cty., IA Part 24, Justice G.C. Aronin. See *AIDS Lit. Rptr.*, January 25, 1991, p. 5698.

56. *Jackie Moore, individually, and as the natural guardian of her minor child, Christopher Case v. Armour Pharmaceutical Co.*, M.D. Fla., Tampa Div., No. 88–392–CIV–T–15C. See *AIDS Lit. Rptr.*, November 23, 1990, p. 5402.

57. *Id.* See *AIDS Lit. Rptr.,* April 26, 1991, p. 6162.

58. *Craig Brogdon v. Miles Laboratories, Inc., Oregon Health Sciences University and Dr. Everett Lovren,* D. Alaska, No. A89-098. See *AIDS Lit. Rptr.,* June 28, 1991, p. 6462.

59. *Moore v. Armour Pharmaceutical Co.,* N.D. Ga., Atlanta Div., No. 1:90-CV-2031-RLV. See *AIDS Lit. Rptr.,* October 12, 1990, p. 5165.

60. *John and Marge McKnight v. American Red Cross et al.,* E.D. Pa., No. 90-7356. See *AIDS Lit. Rptr.,* December 28, 1990, p. 5543.

61. *Neuberger v. Edward Olsen, Administrator of the Estate of Raymond P. Owens,* DE Chanc. Ct., New Castle Cty., No. 12013. See *AIDS Lit. Rptr.,* June 14, 1991, p. 6396.

62. *Rossi v. Estate of Rudolph Almaraz, Johns Hopkins Hospital,* MD Cir. Ct., Baltimore Cty., Nos. 90-344028, CL 123396; *Faya v. Estate of Rudolph Almaraz, Johns Hopkins Hospital,* Nos. 90345011, CL 123459. See *AIDS Lit. Rptr.,* June 28, 1991, p. 6468.

63. *Wogelmuth et al. v. Milton S. Hershey Medical Center of the Pennsylvania State University, Harrisburg Hospital,* PA Ct. of Comm. Pleas, Dauphin Cty., Nos. 2694-S-1991. See *AIDS Lit. Rptr.,* July 26, 1991, p. 6595.

20

Wills

A will is the issue about which most of the inquiries from HIV-infected clients come to attorneys. Having a will is important for a variety of reasons. When a person dies without having formally signed or "executed" a will, state law determines how the person's property will be distributed. In some cases, that distribution is in accord with the way that the deceased person would have wanted his or her estate distributed; in too many other cases, it is not. These state laws do vary, but what is uniform is that the distributions are to lawful relatives by marriage or blood only, with no property going to friends or lovers, no matter what the extent of the relationships and no matter whether the relationships were between persons of the opposite or the same sex.

Other important reasons for having a will relate to the disposition of bodily remains and memorial services. Local medical examiners' offices, hospitals, and funeral homes almost exclusively look to family members for direction on such issues as funeral plans, burial versus cremation, post-funeral possession of the ashes of a cremated deceased, and all of the small decisions involved in each of these issues. Unless there is clear agreement between family members and surviving friends or lovers, the latter are likely to be excluded from the decision-making process at a time when the deceased might have preferred either some degree of sharing in that process or that the decisions be left entirely in the hands of the surviving friend or lover.

Wills are usually not expensive to have written, and the attorney preparing the will can explain the availability of other documents, such as a living will or a power of attorney. Living wills can direct that life not be artificially sustained once there is no hope of recovery. A power of attorney can authorize someone else to take care of an incapacitated person's financial and other affairs during the period of incapacity. Living wills and powers of attorney expire with the death of the person who executed them, and affairs after death can be directed only by a will or similar document that takes effect upon death. An attorney can evaluate the full range of types of documents available so that each person can select the proper ones to effectuate his or her desires. For those leaving substantial amounts of property or having more complicated dispositions or arrangements in mind, an attorney can explain the benefits of a trust and such other alternatives as may be appropriate.

Finally, of these introductory considerations, it is important that a will and related documents be made at a time and under circumstances that do not invite an inference of undue influence. It is on this issue that most of the challenges have arisen, and the cases illustrate how important the timing can be if one wants these documents to be free from suspicion.

Several of the cases in which wills have been contested have involved celebrities. Actress Amanda Blake, who starred for years on the television series "Gunsmoke" and who died of AIDS-related causes in August 1989, executed a new will just three days before she died. The new will cut the inheritances that otherwise would have been due her mother, her sister, and two cousins and instead favored a charity in which Blake had been involved during her final years and the president of which was a longtime friend with whom Blake had lived during her final months. The family contested the will, claiming coercion by the longtime friend. A settlement agreed on by the parties resolved the contest, with the court having endorsed the settlement in February 1990.[1]

Deathbed signatures were alleged in a case where the New York Historical Society was given possession of a dying man's rare silver collection. Noted photographer Robert Mapplethorpe, as the preliminary executor of the estate, alleged that the brain of the owner of the silver collection that was valued as high as $600,000 had been so affected by AIDS that he was unable to understand or comprehend the nature of the contractual arrangements or to make rational judgments concerning particular transactions. The estate and the museum eventually reached a private settlement.[2]

In March 1989, the deathbed will of a California man was set aside pursuant to a jury decision that the deceased had signed it under undue influence and while suffering from AIDS dementia. The will had been executed four days before the man's death, with the claimed undue influence alleged to have been exerted by the deceased lover, who died of AIDS seven months later.[3]

But a Georgia Probate Court jury and judge in February 1989 found valid the will executed by a man one month before his death from AIDS. The suit was brought by the deceased man's father and brother, who were left an 11-year-old Volkswagen and a portion of his jewelry, respectively, and who claimed that the deceased was of diminished mental capacity when he executed the will. The bulk of the estimated $200,000 estate was left instead to the deceased's longtime friend. Testimony of the deceased's own attending physician that the deceased was of sound mind at all relevant times was apparently given greater weight than the contrary testimony of a medical expert on infectious diseases who testified for the family. The latter had based his opinion on medical records that showed no notations that the deceased's mental capacity was reduced. Other testimony came from friends who said that the deceased had felt estranged from his family and had stated openly that he did not want them to receive his estate. The deceased's personal physician corroborated the deceased's statements about the family "rift."[4]

And a New York court ruled that a man was aware of revisions he made to his will less than two months before he died of AIDS, with the court dissolving a temporary restraining order that had prevented distribution of the estate to begin. The deceased had suffered from AIDS dementia and had allegedly been seen engaging in a variety of bizarre acts at the time he changed his will. However, two physicians testified that the man's state of consciousness varied from day to day, and the notaries who were involved in the signings of the changes in the will confirmed that he understood the meaning of the documents. The judge observed that the law on this issue is relatively sparse but, sadly, is likely to increase.[5]

NOTES

1. *Estate of Beverly Louise Neill, also known as Amanda Blake, Louise Neill, et al. v. Performing Animal Welfare Society et al.*, CA Super. Ct., Sacramento Cty., No. 08008, Dept. 18. See *AIDS Lit. Rptr.*, April 13, 1990, p. 4299.

2. *Robert Mapplethorpe as Preliminary Executor of the Estate of Samuel Wagstaff, Jr. v. The New York Historical Society*, NY Sup. Ct., N.Y. Cty., No. 926/88. See *AIDS Lit. Rptr.*, November 11, 1988, p. 1723.

3. *In re Estate of Taylor*, CA Super. Ct., San Francisco Cty., No. 24367/883251. See *AIDS Lit. Rptr.*, March 24, 1989, p. 2426.

4. *In the Matter of David George O'Sheilds*, GA Probate Ct., Fulton Cty., No. 136023. See *AIDS Lit. Rptr.*, February 24, 1989, p. 2273.

5. *Bober et al. v. Harrison et al.*, NY Sup. Ct., N.Y. Cty., IAS Part II, No. 9533/90. See *AIDS Lit. Rptr.*, April 12, 1991, p. 6090.

21

The Americans
with Disabilities Act

As we examined the various subtopics in which there is a relationship between AIDS and the law, we have seen several kinds of laws prohibiting discrimination against PWAs. Recall that the first real protection was found in the employment and public education settings, those protections stemming from Section 504 and related provisions of the federal Rehabilitation Act of 1973.[1]

Section 504 protects against discrimination in programs and activities receiving federal financial assistance; other provisions of the Rehabilitation Act apply the nondiscrimination requirement to federal employment, programs and activities operated by the federal government, and federal contractors.

At the state and local levels, we've seen various degrees of protection for PWAs, with some states having enacted comprehensive statutes to protect the rights of those infected, or even merely perceived as infected with HIV, and other states treating each issue as it arises.

These limited federal and state protections generated the

recognition of a need for more comprehensive and consistent treatment of the rights of the disabled, and from that recognition the Americans with Disabilities Act (ADA) was born.

Signed into law on July 26, 1990, by President Bush, the ADA for the first time provides uniform, enforceable anti-discrimination protections without the need for federal involvement or dollars to be present or special state laws to be enacted.

The ADA very specifically includes people with HIV disease, which is defined to include everything from asymptomatic HIV infection to full AIDS. The ADA also protects from discrimination people who are perceived as having HIV disease, which could include a friend or family member, a lover or caretaker, or a volunteer serving the PWA community.

Probably the most important effect of the ADA will be in the area of employment. The ADA prohibits employers from refusing to hire an applicant, from firing, and from refusing to promote an employee because that person has HIV disease. An employer may not use the fact that an applicant or employee with HIV disease may in the future become too sick to work as an excuse for not hiring the applicant or for firing someone already employed. Similarly, the employer may not use the fact that health care or insurance costs might rise because of the HIV-infected person's employment as justification for refusing to hire the person.[2]

A person must still, of course, be qualified for the job sought. For example, one must be well enough to get to work regularly and to perform adequately all the essential functions of the job, despite the HIV infection.[3]

At the same time, the employer is required to make reasonable accommodations to help employees with disabilities stay on their jobs or applicants with disabilities to get those jobs in the first place. Reasonable accommodations could include such things as flexible work hours, a rest period in the middle of the day, or a bit more than the usual time off for medical appointments.

Note, however, that the employer's obligation is to make

reasonable accommodations and nothing more. An accommodation that would impose an undue hardship on the employer, including a significant expense, might not be required. As with all new laws, the court decisions and implementing regulations will have to help define the parameters of what is and what is not reasonable in terms of accommodations, and this will be done on a case-by-case basis with the size and nature of the employer being important factors.

The ADA treats the testing issue as well. An employer may not require that an employee take an HIV-antibody test unless the employer proves that the test results are necessary for the employee's performance on the job,[4] and recall that with one single exception at only the trial court level, no specific job has yet been held to justify the requirement that an applicant be HIV-negative.

The act does allow the HIV-antibody test to be included in a general physical examination required after a conditional offer of employment is made to a job applicant. But the test may not be selectively administered in a discriminatory manner, and the employer may not withdraw the conditional offer of employment unless the test results indicate that the applicant is no longer qualified for the job.[5]

Beyond employment issues, the ADA further prohibits discrimination based on disability by "public accommodations." That term includes what has traditionally been considered within its meaning—hotels, restaurants, theaters, convention centers, and such. However, the ADA took the term one step further and included within the definition of "public accommodations" virtually every type of business or service provider in the country, including those of doctors, dentists, pharmacists, and, yes, even lawyers.

These public accommodations may not discriminate in the delivery of goods or services against a person because of that person's HIV disease or because the person is regarded as having HIV disease or associates with persons with HIV disease.

These provisions were not easily won. An amendment added by a 12-vote majority in the U.S. House would have given employers the right to remove workers with AIDS from food-handling jobs. ADA backers had expected the Senate to remove the proposal, but a move engineered by Sen. Jesse Helms (R-NC) resulted in formal instructions to that chamber's conferees to support the House-passed amendment. Sen. Edward Kennedy (D-MA) reacted by observing that "if Ryan White were alive and wanted to work at Burger King, this legislation would say no."[6] Sen. Tom Harkin (D-IA), who sponsored the ADA proposal in the Senate, said that the amendment would "codify ignorance" about HIV disease and how it is spread.[7]

The Senate subsequently voted 99 to 1 to let scientific experts determine whether the disease is transmitted by food preparers, directing the U.S. Department of Health and Human Services to publish a list of infectious and communicable diseases that are transmitted through handling of food. The only "no" vote was cast by Helms,[8] and the House ultimately supported that same revision.

Those possibly affected by the ADA's protections should be aware that the law includes a tiered series of effective dates. Employers with more than 25 employees are covered as of July 1992; employers with 15 or more employees are covered as of July 1994. Most of the public accommodations provisions became effective in January 1992, and small places of public accommodations receive yet an additional grace period.[9]

NOTES

1. See "Introduction," n. 21.

2. Feldblum, Chai and Fine, Margaret, "Legislative Update: The Americans with Disabilities Act," a column in "ABA AIDS Network," a publication of the ABA AIDS Coordination Project, Fall 1990, p. 4.

3. *Id.*

4. *Id.*

5. *Id.*

6. "AIDS Patients Could Be Kept from Food Jobs," *The Miami Herald,* June 7, 1990, p. 16A.

7. "Bill Separates AIDS Patients, Food Handling," an Associated Press story appearing in the *Fort Lauderdale Sun-Sentinel,* June 7, 1990, p. 7A.

8. "AIDS, Food-Handling Compromise Reached," *The Miami Herald,* July 12, 1990, p. 15A.

9. See Feldblum, *loc. cit.*

22

The Right to Know

One of the most controversial areas of HIV-related legal issues involves the right of medical service providers to know whether their patients—or prospective patients—are infected with HIV and the right of patients to know whether their medical service providers—or prospective medical service providers—are so infected. There are clearly overlapping issues of confidentiality, testing, and the provision of professional services, but this topic combines those overlapping issues sufficiently to justify a separate treatment.

The issue had been simmering for some time. As is evidenced in Chapter 16, "Public Accommodations and Professional Regulation," fear of exposure to HIV was obviously the primary reason why medical and other service providers turned away prospective patients and customers.

This simmering issue heated up as rumors floated throughout the medical and dental professions that Centers for Disease Control (CDC) was investigating a documentable case of transmission from dentist to patient. By a report published in July 1990, the CDC confirmed rumors that it was investigating the possibility of a transmission of HIV from a dentist who had been diagnosed with AIDS three months before the surgery for extraction of two wisdom teeth to a then-unidentified patient, a 21-year-old college student.[1] Within a few days, the rumor had narrowed the speculation to Florida, and state health department officials were insisting that a confidentiality requirement prohibited them from issuing warnings to the dentist's patients.[2] Inferring that the CDC reports were of her case, the infected patient took steps to sue.[3]

Next and quite dramatically, the dentist identified himself. In an emotional letter released on September 4, 1990, Dr. David J. Acer of Stuart, Florida, said that he did not believe the CDC reports that he may have given AIDS to a patient. He said that he consulted experts after testing positive for HIV antibodies and was assured that he could continue practicing dentistry. "Because I was aware that I had the HIV virus, I was extremely careful in how I practiced dentistry," he said. "I am a gentle man, and I would never intentionally expose anyone to this disease."[4] It turned out that the letter was released the day after Dr. Acer died.

Less than a week later, the patient went public. Then-22-year-old Kimberly Bergalis "stepped before microphones to vent her frustration at the AIDS virus that is killing her and at the dentist . . . she believes infected her."[5] CDC had investigated the case because the health department could not find the source of the infection. The story was front-page news throughout south Florida and in much of the nation. "If I can protect other people from what is happening to me, then I have to do it," Bergalis said.[6] Feature stories correctly compared the media's treatment of the details of her plight to "a tabloid exposé of a beauty queen" or "the trial of a rape victim."[7]

Other patients of Dr. Acer's were tested as the media reported on every new aspect of this issue.[8] From among all those who were tested and who tested positive for HIV without some other factor being identified as the source of the infection, genetic testing "strongly suggested" that Dr. Acer somehow infected three of his patients.[9]

Bergalis ultimately settled her claim against the dentist's insurer for $1 million.[10] She settled her claim against her own insurer, a dental plan that had sent her to Dr. Acer, for an undisclosed sum.[11]

By the time Bergalis had settled both claims, suit had been filed by the other of Dr. Acer's patients whom the CDC genetic testing had suggested were infected by the dentist. The other two were a young married man[12] and a 65-year-old grandmother who had been a Florida "Teacher of the Year."[13] And in early June 1991, the Florida Department of Health and Rehabilitative Services announced that genetic testing by the CDC had linked two more HIV infections of Dr. Acer's patients to the dentist.[14]

And as the cases against Dr. Acer's estate and the dental health insurer that had sent these patients to him became increasingly public, other stories of infected health-care providers began to unfold. In a banner headline of a Sunday edition, the *Baltimore Sun* reported that Johns Hopkins Hospital planned to offer free HIV-antibody tests to patients of a surgeon who specialized in treating women with breast cancer. The surgeon had apparently been exposed to HIV some seven years earlier during an incident of arterial bleeding when he was squirted in the eyes and mouth after making an incision. Estimates were that he had operated on more than 1,800 patients since he joined the hospital's staff just a few months after the exposure.[15] The doctor kept his battle with AIDS "his own personal business, even though his professional business was surgery," the stories reported, as neither the patients nor the employing hospital had been told of the HIV infection prior to the doctor's death.[16] Suits alleging fraud and seeking some $32 million were filed against the estate of the surgeon and his affiliated hospital.[17]

In March 1991, Delaware health officials offered free HIV-antibody tests to more than 1,200 patients of a dentist who died of AIDS-related causes. He had stopped performing riskier dental procedures after he was diagnosed but continued to practice without telling his patients.[18] A former patient filed a class action suit on behalf of all of the deceased dentist's patients and has asked that distribution of the dentist's estate be frozen and a trust fund established to pay for testing and to compensate patients who may have acquired the disease from him through professional contact.[19]

In April 1991, the Children's Hospital Medical Center in Akron, Ohio, notified the parents of dozens of children that a surgeon at the hospital had died of AIDS-related causes and that the youngsters may be at risk. The surgeon reportedly came into contact with fewer than 70 patients because he had been at the hospital in training for only six weeks.[20]

Also in April 1991, a south Florida orthodontist announced in a letter to his patients' parents that he had AIDS. He had continued to practice for three years even though he knew that he had HIV infection.[21] One parent immediately hired the same lawyer who had handled the three cases alleging transmission from Dr. Acer.[22]

In May 1991, prison officials were trying to identify inmates at the Maryland Penitentiary who were treated by a dentist who died of complications from AIDS.[23] Some news reports included rumors that the dentist may not have adhered to CDC recommended infection control measures known as "universal precautions." And at the end of that month, a hospital in Texas notified more than 5,000 former patients that their anesthesiologist had died of complications from AIDS.[24]

And just in case south Florida hadn't already been adequately frightened on this issue, in June 1991, the Veterans' Administration Hospital released the news that one of its dentists at the Oakland Park dental clinic is infected with HIV. It promised to notify patients on whom the dentist had worked and to offer HIV-antibody testing.[25] And in July of that year, a large group of Miami-area patients was notified that their dentist may have worked on them while he had AIDS and that they could get HIV-antibody testing.[26] Medical officials asserted at the earliest of these notices that it would not be unusual for some of this dentist's patients to test positive for HIV antibodies in light of the inner city nature of his practice and the prevalence of AIDS in south Florida.[27]

The list of HIV-infected health-care workers, or those

suspected of being so, continues to grow. In includes, in no special order, an OB-GYN resident at two Harrisburg hospitals;[28] a gynecologist in Boston accused of having had sex with an HIV-infected prostitute;[29] an anesthesiologist and a surgical technician in Bedford, Texas;[30] a dentist in Grand Rapids, Michigan;[31] a dentist in Coran, New York;[32] a dentist in Savannah;[33] a dental student in Chicago;[34] a doctor in Dunkirk, New York;[35] and surely there will be more.

As we look at this topic, several issues should be explored. Among them are

- the medical/dental community's reaction to this issue,
- the validity of the scientific evidence of any alleged transmissions from service provider to patient,
- the level of professional responsibility established and recommended by the several professions involved,
- the risk of infection, and
- the role of regulation by federal and state licensing and regulatory authorities.

As to the reaction of the medical and dental community, it can best be summed up as at least initial disbelief that any transmission has occurred from service provider to patient. Dr. Acer's personal reaction, as contained in his letter to his patients, has already been noted.[36] In a letter to his patients, the south Florida orthodontist who had continued his practice for three years after learning of his infection with HIV said that he followed national CDC guidelines for sterilization and felt "no patients could have been infected by me."[37]

When CDC first issued its report of the then-still anonymous infection of Kimberly Bergalis, a CDC spokesperson said: "We have to assume that this kind of transmission can occur. But we now have about 140,000 AIDS cases, and this is the first one where the question has even come up, so the risk must be awfully small."[38]

Even with that degree of qualification by the CDC, the country's two largest medical associations assailed the CDC report. Scientists from the American Medical Association (AMA) and the American Dental Association (ADA) said that they were skeptical of the link because the CDC could not identify what put the dentist's blood in contact with patient. About a month after the CDC report, the AMA did not accept the link as proven, and the ADA asked the CDC to continue its investigation, which had already probed and discounted any other possible source of infection. The ADA questioned whether there may have been a breakdown in the dentist's infectious-disease prevention techniques.[39]

An investigation using a process called molecular sequencing revealed that the three patients allegedly infected by Dr. Acer had strains of HIV extremely similar to that of the dentist and that those strains were unlike others found in the community.[40] As emphasized by Kimberly Bergalis's attorneys, the data showed a 99.994% probability that Acer infected her with HIV.[41] The findings raised the possibility that contaminated equipment played a role in the transmission.[42] Indeed, further investigation by CDC involved allegations that Acer reused disposable gloves and masks, habitually placed used syringes on a counter in the examining room instead of disposing of them as contaminated instruments and may thereby have reused them,[43] and failed to clean dental tools such as suction equipment between treatments of his patients.[44] There is one theory, frankly given little credibility by those close to the investigation, that Dr. Acer may even have purposely injected his own HIV-tainted blood into patients.[45] The answer simply hasn't yet been found, reported the CDC's Dr. Harold Jaffe at the Sixth International Conference on AIDS in Florence in mid-1991.[46]

The level of professional responsibility established and recommended by the several professions involved is changing as a result of the public examination of these issues. When the Johns Hopkins surgeon's infection became public knowledge on his death, the *Baltimore Sun* ran an analysis of the state of professional obligations at that time. The conclusion: "Ten years into the AIDS epidemic, doctors carrying the AIDS virus remain under no legal obligation to tell their patients they are infected—and ethicists haven't settled the question of whether physicians have the moral obligation to do so."[47] A professor of medical ethics at Georgetown University was quoted as saying that "a physician has a duty to tell patients about those things they would reasonably want to know before establishing a doctor-patient relationship or consenting to a procedure." His guess was that patients would want to know if a surgeon had AIDS before he operated.[48]

But an ethics professor at Marquette University said the risk of spreading the virus "is extremely remote if surgeons wear masks, gloves, and gowns and take other precautions suggested by the federal Centers for Disease Control." He felt that surgeons who take proper precautions are morally obligated to tell their patients only when the disease has reduced their ability to operate competently. At that point, the risk of a surgical mishap heightens, he said.[49]

In January 1991, the AMA and the ADA both announced new guidelines, advising HIV-infected doctors to avoid high-risk procedures without their patients' consent.[50] (Interestingly, the new recommendations were issued the same day as the report from CDC that linked Dr. Acer to the second and third patients.) "[U]ntil the uncertainty about transmission is resolved," the ADA statement said, "HIV-infected dentists should refrain from performing invasive procedures or should disclose their seropositive status." The AMA statement was similar but left open to interpretation the type of invasive procedures that "pose an identifiable risk of transmission." It also called on doctors "at risk of acquiring HIV infection . . . to determine their HIV status." CDC's Dr. Harold Jaffe called the new recommendations "significantly more restrictive."[51]

Taking issue with the AMA and ADA was the New York State Health Department, which said in response to the national groups' statements that health-care workers infected with HIV need not tell their patients their status and may continue to operate or do other invasive procedures.[52] But the Medical Society of New Jersey voted overwhelmingly at its 1991 annual meeting to support mandatory HIV-antibody testing of hospital patients.[53]

CDC had been meeting with representatives of the medical and dental professions ever since its first report in July

1990 on this issue. Some 70 consultants provided input in August 1990, just after the CDC report of the apparent Bergalis transmission.[54]

A two-day meeting was held by CDC in February 1991. The trial balloon was for mandatory HIV-antibody testing for medical service providers, and it met "a chorus of dissent and dismay."[55] Medical workers, union leaders, public health officials, and advocates for people with AIDS joined doctors', dentists', and nurses' associations to warn that testing would be ineffective, unfair, counterproductive, expensive, foolish, cruel, and possibly illegal.

At the February 1991 meetings, the case in favor of mandatory testing focused on infection of only a few patients being too great a risk and a breach of the ethical rule to "do no harm" and was greeted with boos. A representative of the American College of Surgeons warned that such a policy would cut the number of health-care workers willing to risk treating AIDS patients. A representative of the AMA warned that the policy would lead to testing of patients by fearful doctors and that the costs of so much testing would far outweigh any benefits. A doctor from a San Francisco hospital said, "It's time to stop worrying about testing patients or health-care workers and get on with dealing with this epidemic."[56] "If the public were allowed to make policy based on exaggerated fear, no child with HIV would be allowed in school," testified a spokesperson for the American Association of Physicians for Human Rights.[57] The consensus was reported as being that the chances of a patient catching HIV disease from a doctor or dentist are, in the words of a witness from the ACLU's national legislative office, "staggeringly infinitesimal."[58]

By April 1991, CDC had drafted guidelines saying doctors and dentists infected with HIV should get permission from local panels of experts before continuing to perform certain operations and invasive procedures.[59] The guidelines were deemed less restrictive than earlier recommendations from the AMA and the ADA, those recommendations having called for infected health-care professionals to stop performing surgery or inform their patients. The draft guidelines further said that doctors and dentists should heed a professional responsibility to test themselves for HIV.

Focusing on this issue at its 1991 annual meeting, the American Medical Association in late June of that year rejected a policy endorsing mandatory HIV-antibody testing for health-care workers and instead supported voluntary testing of those facing the highest risk.[60] It also reiterated its policy that infected doctors should inform patients or refrain from doing invasive procedures.[61] Within less than three weeks, the Academy of General Dentistry voted at its annual meeting of its approximately 33,000 members to follow federal recommendations that dentists voluntarily take HIV-antibody tests and that those infected with HIV inform their patients. It too declined, however, to urge mandatory testing.[62]

The CDC agreed. Just one day before the Academy's recommendations, the CDC released new guidelines calling for doctors and dentists who perform exposure-prone procedures to submit voluntarily to HIV-antibody tests and that those who test positive refrain from performing exposure-prone procedures until they notify prospective patients and discuss with a board of experts the conditions, if any, under which they ought to resume such operations.[63] It specifically found that "[t]he current assessment of the risk that infected [health-care workers] will transmit HIV . . . to patients during exposure-prone procedures does not support the diversion of resources" that mandatory testing would entail.[64] The parallel to the AMA position was obvious.

"We must get across to the public that in most medical situations there's no more risk from a potential HIV-infected nurse or doctor than from a lawyer, cab driver, or teacher," said the head of the U.S. Public Health Service.[65] Reactions predictably ranged from contempt from the father of Kimberly Bergalis for the refusal to endorse mandatory testing[66] to labeling, by a spokesman for the American Association of Physicians for Human Rights, the CDC action a "medically unjustified witchhunt against HIV-infected health-care workers."[67]

And just what is the risk of infection by a doctor or den-

tist with HIV to a patient? In December 1990, the senior
director for medical affairs at the Johns Hopkins Hospital
stated that 5.3% of health-care workers in the United
States—including aides, nurses, and doctors—have the virus.
Most contracted it sexually or through intravenous drug
use.[68]

"Infection of patients by health-care workers can occur
only during so-called invasive procedures in which body tis-
sues are penetrated by a surgical instrument. For transmission to be possible, the infected surgeon's or dentist's body
fluid must mix with the patient's. Even when all that hap-
pens, the odds of infection appear to be extremely low" according to a *Los Angeles Times* story.[69] CDC calculated the
mathematical risk of an HIV-infected dentist transmitting
the virus to a patient at a range of from one in 263,158 to
one in more than two million, while the risk of dying from a
reaction to anesthesia was calculated at one in 100,000.[70]
Even risk from transmission from surgeons was estimated at
no higher than one in 41,667.[71] It said that as many as 128 or
as few as 13 patients may have contracted the virus from
infected dentists. But the mathematical process of arriving
at even that long shot at HIV infection came under immediate attack. The ADA called the numbers "unrealistically
high."[72]

Beyond those attempts at actual calculations, the obser-
vations of many in both the health-care professions and in
the regulation of them have echoed the word used by the
ACLU's lobbyist on this issue. "[I]nfinitesimal, as long as
proper infection control procedures are followed," said one
spokesman for the American Dental Association in June
1991.[73] "[I]nfinitesimal as long as universal precautions are
followed," said an executive of that same association a
month later.[74] "As individuals we all want the most risk-free
environment, but the risk is already infinitesimal," said the
president of the American Foundation for AIDS Research.[75]
"The risk of getting AIDS from your doctor is lower than the
risk of dying in a car crash on the way to the hospital," said
the Assistant Secretary for Health at the U.S. Department of
Health and Human Services.[76]

What about the other side of possible transmission? Studies examining the risk to health-care workers from infected patients estimate that only 0.4% of all needle sticks involving contaminated blood have resulted in infection.[77]

Let's look at some harder numbers. An August 1990 estimate by the ADA was that 4,500 health-care workers in the United States were then infected with HIV, some 144 of them being dentists.[78] As of December 31, 1990, CDC had documented 5,815 health-care workers with HIV disease. Of those, 156 were dental workers—mostly dentists—and 42 were surgeons.[79] Of 3,420 orthopedic surgeons tested for HIV antibodies at the March 1991 convention of the American Academy of Orthopedic Surgeons, only two were found to be infected with the virus, and neither of them was practicing.[80] By the time the new CDC guidelines were issued, the estimates had grown to nearly 6,800 health-care workers being infected with HIV, 170 of them being dentists or dental hygienists and another 730 being physicians.[81]

Perhaps more important numbers, though, are these. When a surgeon died of complications of AIDS with a suggested infection date of as early as January 1, 1982, the Tennessee Department of Health and the Environment wrote to all patients on whom he had operated after that date and offered free HIV-antibody testing. Of 616 patients tested, only one was positive, and he was an intravenous drug user.[82] Of the Johns Hopkins surgeon's patients who were tested, of the Delaware dentist's patients who were tested, of the Ohio surgeon's patients who were tested, of the south Florida orthodontist's patients who were tested, there are *no reports* of alleged HIV transmission from the infected medical worker. Of the other, more recent reports on which fewer tests have as yet been run, still none of the patients suggested transmission from the infected medical worker. After all of this study and all these tests—after more than 170,000 cases of HIV disease have been reported since the disease was discovered in 1981—the only alleged incidents of transmission from medical worker to patient are the five attributed to Dr. Acer.[83] Too few, however, examine the issue with that degree of realism.

As was pointed out in an editorial in the daily newspaper that serves the distressed population in the area where Dr. Acer and the south Florida orthodontist practiced, mandatory testing is a costly response that wouldn't necessarily offer more protection than the ethical, voluntary actions called for by the AMA and ADA. Not only is the chance of transmission very low, but there are false positive tests, a "window period" during which the antibodies are not detected by current tests, and other false negative tests.[84] And as was noted in Chapter 18, "Testing," the prospect of required testing, particularly when coupled with named-identified reporting or contact tracing, drives underground many who are most in need of the testing, diagnosis, and treatment system.

The Oregon Medical Association adopted a policy similar to the AMA recommendations. It requires doctors infected with HIV to advise the State Health Division. A group of peers would then decide whether an infected doctor poses a risk to patients and whether the doctor's medical license should be limited.[85] Similarly, under legislation enacted in 1991, state medical boards and the Florida Department of Health and Rehabilitative Services will be allowed to set guidelines in that state for health-care professionals with HIV disease.[86] Idaho took a somewhat different approach, adopting rules that allow emergency health-care workers to be told if they handle people who test positive for HIV antibodies.[87] The Illinois legislature enacted a new law in 1991 to authorize the state's health department to notify patients when their medical-care providers are diagnosed with AIDS. According to *Time* magazine, the bill was prompted by the revelation that the only dentist in a town of 2,700 people had died of AIDS in late 1990.[88]

Other states have taken off in assorted directions. The governor of Maryland proposed HIV-antibody testing for all patients undergoing high-risk procedures as well as for health-care workers engaged in those procedures.[89] The New Jersey Board of Medical Examiners said in an advisory opinion that HIV-positive physicians should refrain from performing surgery and that doctors who think they may be

HIV-positive should take antibody tests.[90] In Georgia, the license of a Savannah dentist was suspended on the basis of a colleague's assertion that the dentist was mentally impaired from AIDS.[91] And an Anderson, Indiana, dentist had his license suspended after the media reported him as being HIV-infected. His license was restored but only after a promise that he would not practice until he recovers from a mild stroke.[92]

State health officials in Connecticut, however, rejected calls for HIV-antibody testing of patients of an orthodontist who had died of complications from AIDS but who was careful to use infection control procedures.[93]

The case for the right of either medical/dental service providers or patients to demand testing in order to know whether the other may be infected with HIV is extremely weak. Consider the damage likely to be done to the medical/dental practices of those who adhere to the CDC recommended universal precautions, the availability of the already too few practitioners willing to examine and treat those patients who know that they are or may be HIV-positive, and the process of bringing those who may have been exposed to the virus into the examination, counseling, testing, and treatment process. It would surely seem that strict enforcement of infection-control measures and implementation of the universal precautions recommended by CDC would be the far better solution.

Congress is also considering how to react on this issue. Just days after the CDC issued its July 1991 guidelines, the Senate passed by a 99–0 vote a measure pressuring states to require health-care workers who perform high-risk treatments involving exposure to blood to undergo AIDS-antibody testing. Those who are HIV-positive would have to notify patients or stop treating them.[94] Far more extreme, though, was a measure passed by a Senate vote of 81–18 on the same day. If enacted into law, it would set criminal penalties of up to ten years in jail for HIV-infected health-care workers who know they have the virus and continue to treat patients without notifying them.[95] One national newspaper termed Senate passage of these bills "bowing to public fears about AIDS."[96] One Senator who opposed the criminal penalties bill called it "a double sentencing," saying that health-care workers who test positive "die twice—once professionally and then from AIDS."[97] Nearly every story that carried the arguments of opposing Senators or the positions of such opposing organizations as the AMA also carried the warning of sponsoring Senator Jesse Helms: "Don't try to tell that to Kimberly Bergalis."[98]

As one looks at this question of testing, a factor that simply cannot be ignored is cost. A July 1991 report by the Pennsylvania state health department estimated that it would cost $54 million annually to conduct quarterly testing of the state's health-care workers for HIV, an amount more than twice the total Pennsylvania AIDS-prevention program budget.[99] Another 1991 study found that the cost of even onetime testing with pre- and post-test counseling for health-care workers at San Francisco General Hospital would be approximately $886,000, twice the entire infection control annual budget for that hospital.[100] A 1991 study by the AIDS Policy Center found that if the seven million health-care workers in the United States were tested for HIV and hepatitis B, it would cost between $350 and $525 million.[101]

As *Newsweek* asked in its analysis,[102] where would disclosure end? "Should a physician with a seizure disorder tell his patient about his condition?" What about doctors who are recovering alcoholics or substance abusers? It quoted one epidemiologist who asked, "Do you have to tell the patient you had a fight with your wife this morning and it is affecting your judgment?"[103]

And if there is to be disclosure, what will happen to those health-care workers who have or acquire HIV? The *Newsweek* analysis concluded that they could become activists; they could work in noninvasive fields like psychiatry; they could limit their practices to people with AIDS, for whom the available medical care is clearly at a reduced level than for others; or they could continue to practice, "keeping their painful secret."[104]

Beyond that, what will happen to the health-care system

if mandatory testing or disclosure become law? With testing HIV-positive generally meaning an end to a health-care worker's career as it had been, one can easily foresee that health-care workers will be far less willing to risk infection by treating those known to be, or suspected of being, HIV-positive. That means all who are already infected will have less care available, and infected health-care workers will surely "go underground." The decrease in willingness to expose oneself to HIV also means that fewer health-care workers will be willing to work in those settings where exposure to HIV is more likely—clinics and emergency rooms. And a reduction in clinical and emergency room settings clearly would have an impact on the nation's poor and a disparate impact on minorities. Such testing and disclosure portend a health-care system with care available only, or at least in better quantity and quality, for those with middle and upper incomes, those who are white, those who are (or at least appear to be) straight. One must ask the hopefully rhetorical question of whether that is what America is supposed to be about!

NOTES

1. "Report: Dentist May Have Passed AIDS on to Patient," a Herald Wire Services story in *The Miami Herald,* July 27, 1990, p. 18A.

2. "Patient Who Contracted AIDS at Dentist's Is Floridian," a Chicago Tribune story appearing in the *Fort Lauderdale Sun-Sentinel,* July 29, 1990, p. 20A.

3. "Florida Woman to Sue Dentist in AIDS case," a Knight-Ridder News Service story appearing in *The Miami Herald,* August 29, 1990, p. 2B.

4. "Dentist with AIDS Urges Former Patients to Be Tested," an Associated Press story appearing in *The Miami Herald,* September 5, 1990, p. 5B.

5. "AIDS Patient Goes Public, Blames Dentist," *The Miami Herald,* September 8, 1990, p. 1A.

6. "Woman Sues Dentist's Estate, Says Treatment Gave Her AIDS," *Fort Lauderdale Sun-Sentinel,* September 8, 1990, p. 1A.

7. "Positive," *Fort Lauderdale Sun-Sentinel,* September 26, 1990, p. 1E.

8. "Dentist's Patients Are Tested," *Fort Lauderdale Sun-Sentinel,* October 1, 1990, p. 8B.

9. "Federal Report Links Stuart Dentist's Hygiene to 3 AIDS Infections," *The Miami Herald,* January 17, 1991, p. 1A.

10. *Bergalis v. CNA Insurance Co.,* FL Cir. Ct., Martin Cty. See *AIDS Lit. Rptr.,* January 25, 1991, p. 5693, and "AIDS Patient Settles Claim Against Estate of Dentist," *The Miami Herald,* January 23, 1991, p. 1A.

11. *Bergalis v. CIGNA Dental Health of Florida,* FL Cir. Ct., Martin Cty., No. 91–123–CA. See *AIDS Lit. Rptr.,* April 12, 1991, p. 6087, and "AIDS Victim Settles Insurance Suit," *The Miami Herald,* p. 4B.

12. *Richard and Deanne Driskill et al. v. CIGNA Dental Health of Florida, Inc.,* FL Cir. Ct., Martin Cty., No. 91 177 CA-Makemson. See *AIDS Lit. Rptr.,* February 22, 1991, p. 5847.

13. *Barbara C. Webb and Robert H. Webb v. CIGNA Dental Health of Florida, Inc.,* FL Cir. Ct., Martin Cty., No. 91 280 CA. See *AIDS Lit. Rptr.,* March 22, 1991, p. 6004.

14. "Two More AIDS Cases Linked to Stuart Dentist," *The Miami Herald,* June 7, 1991, p. 1A.

15. "Hopkins to Alert Patients of Doctor Who Died of AIDS," *Baltimore Sun,* December 2, 1990, p. 1A.

16. "Surgeon with AIDS Kept Illness Secret," *The Miami Herald,* December 9, 1990, p. 10A.

17. *Rossi v. Estate of Rudolph Almaraz, Johns Hopkins Hospital,* MD Cir. Ct., Baltimore Cty., No. 90–344028, CL 123396, HCAO No. 90–447. See *AIDS Lit. Rptr.,* January 25, 1991, p. 5702.

18. "Delaware Offers Free AIDS Test to Dentist's Patients," an Associated Press story appearing in *The Miami Herald,* March 17, 1991, p. 7A.

19. *Neuberger v. Edward Olsen, Administrator of the Estate of Raymond P. Owens,* DE Chancery Ct., New Castle Cty., No. 12013. See *AIDS Lit. Rptr.,* April 12, 1991, p. 6093.

20. "Surgeon Has AIDS," *Fort Lauderdale Sun-Sentinel,* April 11, 1991, p. 3A.

21. "AIDS Orthodontist Had the Virus Since 1988, Lawyer Says," *The Miami Herald,* April 18, 1991, p. 1BR.

22. "Orthodontist Has AIDS, Parents Learn by Letter," *The Miami Herald,* April 17, 1991, p. 1A.

23. *The Miami Herald,* May 23, 1991, p. 4A.

24. *The Miami Herald,* June 2, 1991, p. 11A, and June 4, 1991, p. 11A.

25. "Broward VA: Dentist Has AIDS Virus," *The Miami Herald,* June 5, 1991, p. 1A.

26. "HRS Testing Patients of Dentist with AIDS," *The Miami Herald,* July 24, 1991, p. 1B.

27. "Dr. Melton White, Miami Dentist Suffering from AIDS," *The Miami Herald,* August 3, 1991, p. 4B.

28. "M.D. infected; 442 told," *Fort Lauderdale Sun Sentinel,* June 20, 1991, p. 3A.

29. "Statesline," *USA Today,* June 26, 1991, p. 10A.

30. *The Advocate,* No. 581 (July 16, 1991), p. 34.

31. *The Advocate,* No. 581 (July 16, 1991), p. 33.

32. "Statesline," *USA Today,* July 17, 1991, p. 11A.

33. "Bryan May Test for AIDS," *Savannah Evening Press,* July 15, 1991, p. 1.

34. *Fort Lauderdale Sun-Sentinel,* July 24, 1991, p. 3A.

35. "Doctor with AIDS Virus Evokes Anger and Pathos," *New York Times,* July 29, 1991, p. B1.

36. See n. 4, *supra.*

37. See n. 21, *supra.*

38. "Dentist-Patient AIDS Case Questioned," *The Miami Herald,* July 28, 1990, p. 14A.

39. "AIDS Link to Dentist in Florida Challenged," *The Miami Herald,* September 14, 1990, p. 1A.

40. "Dental Equipment, AIDS Link Weighed," a Los Angeles Times story appearing in the *Fort Lauderdale Sun-Sentinel,* January 11, 1991, p. 4A.

41. See *AIDS Lit. Rptr.,* March 22, 1991, p. 6004.

42. See n. 40, *supra.*

43. "How Could AIDS Pass From Dentist?," *Fort Lauderdale Sun-Sentinel,* July 1, 1991, p. 1D.

44. "Dentist's Needles, AIDS May be Linked," *Palm Beach Post,* January 17, 1991, p. 1B.

45. "Investigators Uncover Clues on HIV Transmission in Florida Dentist's Office," *The Advocate,* No. 585 (September 10, 1991), p. 44.

46. "How Detective Tried to Unravel AIDS Mystery," *The Miami Herald,* June 23, 1991, p. 7B.

47. "No Ethics Guides Exist for Doctors Who Have AIDS," *Baltimore Sun,* December 2, 1990, p. 10A.

48. *Id.*

49. Id.

50. "Guidelines Issued for Doctors with AIDS," *The Miami Herald*, January 18, 1991, p. 1A.

51. *Id.*

52. "State: Doctors Needn't Disclose AIDS Virus," *The Miami Herald*, January 19, 1991, p. 2A.

53. "New Jersey Physicians Speed Nationwide Push for Forced HIV Tests," *The Advocate*, No. 578 (June 4, 1991), pp. 14–15.

54. "Dentist's AIDS Case Spurs Talk of Controls," a Los Angeles Times story appearing in the *Ft. Lauderdale Sun-Sentinel*, October 21, 1990, p. 7H.

55. "Reject AIDS Tests for Health Workers, Doctors Tell CDC," *The Miami Herald*, February 22, 1991, p. 8A.

56. *Id.*

57. "Health-Care Professionals Oppose AIDS Disclosures," *Fort Lauderdale Sun-Sentinel*, February 22, 1991, p. 4A.

58. *Id.*

59. "Agency Drafts Guidelines for Doctors with AIDS," a New York Times story appearing in the *Fort Lauderdale Sun-Sentinel*, April 5, 1991, p. 6A.

60. "AMA Votes Down Mandatory AIDS Testing," an Associated Press story appearing in *The Miami Herald*, June 27, 1991, p. 10A.

61. "AMA Rejects Mandatory AIDS Testing," *USA Today*, June 27, 1991, p. 1A.

62. "Dentists OK Voluntary AIDS Tests," an Associated Press story in the *Fort Lauderdale Sun-Sentinel*, July 17, 1991, p. 3A.

63. "CDC Officials Urge Doctors, Dentists to Take AIDS Tests," *Fort Lauderdale Sun-Sentinel*, July 16, 1991, p. 1A.

64. "Recommendations for Preventing Transmission of Human Immunodeficiency Virus and Hepatitis B Virus to Patients During Exposure-Prone Invasive Procedures," *Morbidity and Mortality Weekly Report*, Vol. 40, No. RR–8, July 12, 1991.

65. "AIDS Test Urged for Health Workers," *The Miami Herald*, July 16, 1991, p. 1A.

66. See n. 63, *supra.*

67. "Voluntary HIV Tests Urged for Health Workers," *USA Today*, July 16, 1991, p. 1D.

68. "Risk of Infection in Health Care Small," *Baltimore Sun*, December 2, 1990, p. 10A.

69. See n. 54, *supra.*

70. "CDC Calculates Risk of Dentists Infecting Patients with AIDS," *The Miami Herald,* February 7, 1991, p. 8A.

71. See n. 57, *supra.*

72. See n. 70, *supra.*

73. "Ill Dentist Must Have Been Woefully Lax, Expert Says," an Associated Press story appearing in *The Miami Herald,* June 14, 1991, p. 4B.

74. "AIDS Risk to Patients Seen as Slim," *The Miami Herald,* July 13, 1991, p. 1BR.

75. See n. 65, *supra.*

76. "Should You Worry About Getting AIDS From Your Dentist?," *Time,* July 29, 1991, p. 50.

77. See n. 54, *supra.*

78. "PBC Woman Claims Dentist with AIDS Infected Her in Visit," *Fort Lauderdale Sun-Sentinel,* August 29, 1990, p. 7B.

79. See n. 70, *supra.*

80. "Few Surgeons Test Positive at Meeting," *The Miami Herald,* May 17, 1991, p. 18A. See *Morbidity and Mortality Report,* May 17, 1991, p. 309.

81. See n. 76, *supra.*

82. See n. 68, *supra.*

83. See n. 59 and n. 14, *supra.*

84. "Doctors, Heal Thyselves; Volunteer for AIDS Test," *Palm Beach Post,* January 24, 1991, p. E1.

85. "Group Adopts Policy for Doctors with AIDS," *The Miami Herald,* April 29, 1991, p. 10A.

86. "AIDS Bill Passes," *The Miami Herald,* May 2, 1991, p. 12A.

87. See n. 53, *supra.*

88. See n. 76, *supra.*

89. "Governor Draws Praise, Scorn for AIDS-Testing Plan," *Baltimore Sun,* August 7, 1991, p. 1B.

90. *The Advocate,* No. 581 (July 16, 1991), p. 33.

91. "The AIDS Media Circus," *The Advocate,* No. 585 (September 10, 1991), p. 32 et seq., at 36.

92. *Id.*

93. *The Advocate,* No. 583 (August 13, 1991), p. 22.

94. "AIDS Tests for Doctors get Boost," *The Miami Herald,* July 19, 1991, p. 1A.

95. *Id.*

96. "Senate Gets 'Tough' on HIV Disclosure," *USA Today,* July 19–21, 1991, p. 1A.

97. *Id.*

98. *Id.*

99. "Mandatory HIV Testing Intensifies Across America," *The Advocate,* No. 585 (September 10, 1991), p. 40.

100. *Id.*

101. *Id.*

102. "Doctors and AIDS," *Newsweek,* July 1, 1991, pp. 48 *et seq.,* at 54.

103. *Id.*

104. *Id.,* at 56.

Glossary

AIDS

The acronym for Acquired Immune Deficiency Syndrome, a viral disease that impairs the body's ability to fight disease.

ARC

The acronym for AIDS-Related Complex, a stage of HIV disease in which the virus is present but symptoms do not include life-threatening opportunistic infections that mark full AIDS.

Antibodies

Proteins made by the body to defend against foreign organisms or toxins. HIV antibodies are ineffective in that regard but do signal the presence of HIV.

Appellate Court

Any court above the trial court in either the state or federal court system; it hears cases on appeal from the trial court.

Defendant

The person or entity against whom or which suit is brought.

CDC	The acronym for the U.S. Centers for Disease Control.
ELISA Test	The basic test that indicates the presence of HIV antibodies.
HIV	The acronym for Human Immunodeficiency Virus, the virus believed to cause AIDS.
HIV-negative	Having an absence of HIV antibodies detected by blood testing.
HIV-positive	Having the presence of HIV antibodies detected by blood testing.
Opportunistic Infection	Medical problems that do not usually occur in persons with healthy immune systems.
Plaintiff	The person or entity bringing suit.
PWA	The acronym for a person with AIDS. (PLWA, person living with AIDS, is used by some instead of PWA.)
Trial Court	That court in either the state or federal court system in which the case or matter is originally heard or tried.
Universal Precautions	Guidelines recommended by the CDC so that medical and dental service providers can avoid risking transmission of infectious disease, including HIV disease.